More Money
Than God

More Money Than God

LIVING A RICH LIFE WITHOUT LOSING YOUR SOUL

Steven Z. Leder

bonus books

Chicago and Los Angeles

07 06 05 04   5 4 3 2

Library of Congress Control Number: 2003112838

Permissions:
From *UH-OH* by Robert Fulghum., copyright © 1991 by Robert Fulghum. Used by permission of Villard Books, a division of Ran-dom House, Inc.

Max, Aggie. 1997. "The Bag Lady and the Banquet," *Salon.com*, *www.salon.com/july97/mothers/aggie970722.html*, excerpted from *The Last Resort: Scenes from a Transient Hotel* (San Fran-cisco, Chronicle Books).

Bonus Books
875 N. Michigan Ave.
Suite 1416
Chicago, IL 60611

Printed in the United States of America

To my parents, Leonard and Barbara Leder

*"A baby enters the world with hands clenched,
as if to say, 'The world is mine; I shall grab it.'
A person leaves with hands open, as if to say,
'I can take nothing with me.' "*

—ECCLESIASTES RABBAH

‖ Contents

‖ Acknowledgments

‖ I AM GRATEFUL TO MANY PEO-
ple without whom this book never would have been written. My heartfelt thanks to my agent Linda Konner for
trusting me with a great idea and for partnering me with
Jodie Gould, who was a pleasure to work with on this
manuscript, and without whom it never would have been
finished. I want to thank my friend Steve Sigoloff for
bringing me to the attention of Jeff Stern at Bonus Books.
I want to thank Jeff Stern for his faith in me and his fine
staff at Bonus Books, including Kelley Thornton and
Stephanie Adams. To the many members of Wilshire
Boulevard Temple, who willingly have shared their lives
with me as their rabbi and their friend. The fruit of that
sharing is on every page of this book and my life. The
deepest thanks goes to my wife Betsy and to my children,
Aaron and Hannah, who teach me every day how rich
and blessed I am.

|| Introduction

A SAGE WAS ASKED: "WHOM DO YOU
BELIEVE ARE GREATER, THE WISE OR
THE RICH?"

"THE WISE," THE SAGE ANSWERED.

"BUT IF THAT IS THE CASE, WHY DO YOU
FIND MORE OF THE WISE AT THE DOORS
OF THE WEALTHY RATHER THAN THE
WEALTHY AT THE DOORS OF THE WISE?"

"BECAUSE THE WISE APPRECIATE THE
VALUE OF RICHES, BUT THE RICH DO
NOT ALWAYS SIMILARLY APPRECIATE THE
VALUE OF WISDOM."

—SOLOMON'S PEARLS OF WISDOM

|| WHEN I FIRST GOT THE IDEA
to write a book about money, America was in the midst of
the greatest economic boom in recent history. At the time,
we had experienced a decade of continuous growth, fueled
in part by a soaring stock market. According to New York
University economics professor Edward N. Wolff, the number of American households worth ten million dollars or
more had quadrupled during this period.

All this produced unimagined wealth for many people, including those who were barely old enough to toast their newfound fortune. It got me thinking: what are the attendant spiritual problems that come with having "more money than God"—that is to say, more money than any person ever could need? And what about those who feel they are smart enough and work hard enough to be rich, but somehow have missed the party? How much is too much? How much is enough?

Even though America's fortunes are not what they used to be, the economy is sure to crest and dip like the waves of the ocean. Whatever our economic status may be at the moment, money issues always will permeate our lives, and souls, if we let them. Ironically, the problem, as the philosopher Jacob Needleman recognized, is not that we take money too seriously, but that we do not take it seriously enough. Economist John Maynard Keynes observed, "To me it seems clearer every day that the moral problem of our age is concerned with the love of money, with the habitual appeal to the money motive in nine-tenths of the activities in life."

Money itself is not evil. As one of the Bible's most misquoted passages says, it is the *love* of money that is the cause of wickedness. Money can be the source of good through charitable giving and as funding for community programs, or it can encourage selfish and evil acts. For many of us, the most noble and the most immoral things we will ever do in our lives will involve the use or misuse of money.

More Money Than God will examine how money impacts our families, friends, work, loves, ethics, compulsions, and feelings of self-worth. There's an old Yiddish curse that says, "May you be very wealthy and the only one in your family that is." I have seen money tear families apart or bring two people together who don't belong as a couple. Just tune into any courtroom TV show and you will see husbands and wives, sisters and brothers, mothers and daughters battling over a few measly bucks. Was Shakespeare's Polonius right when he advised his son, "Neither a borrower nor a lender be"?

Money can be either a tool for teaching our children important moral principles or the instrument for producing spoiled, slothful adults. My family and I live on a rabbi's salary in Los Angeles, California, surrounded by people who are extremely wealthy. Some of my congregants own private jets. While my children understand that wealth is a wonderful thing, I have taught them that it is not what we are put on Earth to seek. They realize that meaningful work is more important than lucrative work. They know this because I tell them over and over again and because I live the example every day of my life.

This book is not about how to get rich. I'm a spiritual adviser, not a financial one. But it will tell you how to balance your life as carefully as your bank account. I will show you why money and spirituality are not mutually exclusive and, as many unscrupulous business leaders have discovered, why you must conduct your business affairs as if God is the ultimate CEO.

Money, I believe, is neither good nor bad. It's how you earn it, what you *do* with it, and how you treat others who are less fortunate, that's important. Once we start to believe that we are better than others are simply because we are wealthier, our souls are on their way to becoming coarse and shallow. There is a kind of nobility in knowing how to use money wisely and for the greater good. As the nineteenth-century preacher Henry Ward Beecher once said, "Some of God's noblest sons will be selected from those who know how to take wealth, with all its temptations, and maintain godliness therewith. It is hard to be a saint standing in a golden niche."

Even the word *fortune* indicates that there is an element of luck in being rich. Some are born into money, some marry into it, and some have money dropped into their laps through nepotism, inheritance, or savvy investments. Does this make them better or just luckier? Whether you worked hard for your money or got it through a trust fund, I will explain why all of us must devote at least a portion of our time and resources to helping others.

This book will also help you to understand the difference between your wants and your needs. In my experience as a clergyman, most people whose lives are out of balance got that way because they started to believe they needed what they wanted. My wife and I learned this when the closing for the home we wanted fell through. Because we already had sold the house in which we were living, we had to rent a very small, two-bedroom apartment to share with two kids and a dog. Given the real estate situation in Los Angeles, we might have had to wait anywhere from two months to two years before finding a home that we could afford.

During our move into smaller quarters, we were forced to take inventory of all the things we owned and evaluate their value and importance to us. To our surprise, we found that we needed only about 10 percent of what we had. We ended up taking our clothing, a sofa, a table, two chairs, a television, dishes, a couple of beds, and a computer—that's about it. Could it be that 90 percent of what we spend our time and energy amassing is unnecessary? Do we really need what we want?

And finally, what kind of moral code do we need to live by while seeking the comfort that money brings? Ironically, putting money into perspective allows us to fully appreciate its worth and to create a spiritual paradigm for becoming a successful person with a full, rich life. God has created a universe filled with a bounty of nature and companionship. It is a bounty that we all share, whether we are a "have" or a "have not."

So live well and prosper. And, with the help of this book, take inventory of what you have achieved up to now. You probably have more than you realize. Keep in mind what a wise rabbi once said as he saw a man hurrying along the street:

> "Why are you rushing so much?" he asked the harried man.
>
> "I'm rushing after my livelihood," the man answered.
>
> "How do you know," asked the rabbi, "that your livelihood is running on before you so that you have to rush after it? Perhaps it is behind you, and all you need to do is stand still."

CHAPTER ONE | # Who Wants to Be a Millionaire?

A POOR MAN IS WALKING IN THE FOR-
EST CONVERSING WITH GOD. HE ASKS,
"LORD, WHAT IS A MILLION YEARS TO
YOU?"

GOD REPLIES, "MY SON, A MILLION
YEARS IS LIKE A SECOND TO ME."

THE MAN THEN ASKS, "LORD, WHAT
IS A MILLION DOLLARS TO YOU?"

GOD REPLIES, "MY SON, A
MILLION DOLLARS IS LESS THAN
A PENNY TO ME."

THE MAN STORES UP HIS COURAGE
AND ASKS, "SO GOD, CAN I HAVE A
MILLION DOLLARS?"

TO WHICH GOD REPLIES: "IN A
SECOND."

—101 CLASSIC JEWISH JOKES

‖ **WHO WANTS TO BE A MILLION-** aire? A silly question, perhaps. As money wizard Andrew Tobias said, that's like asking who wants to be good-looking. Still, if a genie gave you the choice between riches or beauty, which would you choose? Most people would probably pick wealth. As we all know, beauty fades, but money earns interest with time.

Many of us of us who don't have a lot of money want to get rich, preferably while we're still young and, even better, overnight. Despite the fact that the dot-com money has burned up, a lot of people still think they can strike it rich if only they pick the right stock, the right number, or, last and least preferable, work hard enough.

The idea that anyone can be rich as long as he or she works hard is an old American dream. For many, this has been replaced with the new American dream—to get rich quickly with the least amount of effort. Money no longer represents a job well done. It no longer represents effort or commitment. The possibility of making money—gobs of it—without actually having to work for it is why we have casinos, sweepstakes, and TV shows like *Survivor*. They feed into this frenzied notion that a million dollars is simply a contest away.

Part of our money lust comes from the changing image of what it means to be a millionaire. During the late sixties, young people eschewed materialism for more idealistic pursuits like civil rights, women's rights, and peace. During the eighties, we saw the coke-snorting greed-is-gooders on Wall Street as empty, valueless creatures.

When the Internet boom hit during the early nineties, the dot-comers, whom we viewed as cyber pioneers, became young millionaires. For a time they could thumb their noses at the corporate establishment even as they became consumed by it. Wealth was the talisman that allowed us to strip off our stodgy white shirts and ties in favor of jeans and T-shirts. Money was hip again.

Then came the crash. Shortly after we crossed the threshold into the new millennium, we saw the Internet take a nosedive. Executives from Enron, Imclone, World-Com, Tyco, Arthur Anderson, and others got caught in the headlights of deceit and corruption. On September 11, 2001, we saw our old world of insulated innocence and comfort crumble as thousands died tragically at the hands of terrorists.

How has this confluence of events changed our worldview? For one, we are reassessing the role that money plays in our lives. Today, we have a more realistic understanding about what it takes to become a millionaire and to what degree we are willing to sacrifice our lives in order to be rich.

The overwhelming desire for wealth is a bit like an average person wanting to be a model or professional athlete. The next time you're at the supermarket checkout line, take a look at the women's magazines. Most feature models with impossibly perfect figures and articles on how to transform your ordinary self into something worthy of those same magazine covers. And for every woman's magazine with an article on weight loss, there are articles for men on superstar athletes and investors. We measure ourselves against an almost superhuman standard of beauty and physical perfection. What we often forget is that very few people are born with beauty and athletic prowess; the rest of us have to work at it and be satisfied with modest results.

Are you willing to live the way one has to live in order to look like Catherine Zeta-Jones or to compete in the Olympics? Do you want to give up the food you eat, subject yourself to plastic surgery, or train for hours every day? And even if you did, could you really accomplish your goal? Maybe deep down what we all need most is the ability to make peace with what God and DNA have given us.

The same can be said about the pursuit of wealth. Are you willing to invest the time and energy it takes to make more money? For most people, accumulating wealth still means long hours and hard work. Money is difficult to amass in large amounts, and the demands that enable people to make a lot of money are great. If it were easy, everyone would be rich!

Younger people, especially, have been forced to change their perception of money. Prior to the Internet boom, many assumed that they could graduate from college, work for a start-up, get paid in stock options, and convert it all into cash. They could be millionaires, at least on paper. Now, these same eager graduates must put on business suits, tuck their resumes into their brief-cases, and pound the proverbial pavement, often for an entry-level job. The good news, as Michael Lewis, chronicler of young business titans optimistically ob-served, is that young people might now pursue jobs they enjoy rather than those that will simply make them wealthy. We shall see.

In a speech to a graduating class of high school stu-dents, author Robert Fulghum asked how many would like to be an adult—an independent, on-your-own citizen:

> All would raise their hands with some enthusiasm. And then I would give them a list of things grown-ups do: Clean the sink strainer. Plunge out the toi-let. Clean up babies when they poop and pee. Wipe runny noses and other orifices. Clean ovens and grease traps and roasting pans. Empty the kitty box and scrape up the dog doo. Carry out the garbage. Bury dead animals when they get run over in the street. When you are a kid, you feel that if they re-ally loved you, your folks wouldn't ever ask you to take out the garbage. When you join the ranks of the grown-ups, you take out the garbage because you love them. And by them, I mean not only your own family, but the family of human kind.

Fulghum is right. We must all learn how to do at least some of the dirty work. The Hebrew word for sacrifice is *korban*. It comes from the word *karov*, which means to "draw close" or "to come near." It's true that we feel closest to the things for which we sacrifice: our careers, our home, our children, our parents, our lovers.

If we want more out of life, we must put more in. If we want a better marriage, we have to give more of ourselves. If we want a better world, we have to give more of our money and our time. If we want wisdom, we have to take the time to read and to learn. If we want a more spiritual life, we must take the time for prayer, meditation, church, or synagogue. If we want more money, we have to work and sacrifice for it.

A life that demands nothing from us, that seeks to merely accommodate our laziness, our preoccupation with things shiny and new, and our shallow pursuits—a life devoid of sacrifice—will bring us nothing in return. If we want the dividends that life can bring, we have to invest the emotional capital, the educational capital, and the spiritual capital. We have to do the hard, sweaty, dirty work.

When violinist Isaac Stern concluded a concert recital one evening, he was approached by an ardent fan who gushed: "Oh, Mr. Stern, I would give anything to be able to play the violin is magnificently as you do!" To which the maestro softly replied, "Would you give twelve hours a day?"

MONEY WORSHIP

No matter how much or how little you have at the moment, you must consider whether money is the focal point of your life. We live in a consumer-driven, capitalistic society, so it is difficult to be immune to the desire for wealth. Besides, Americans believe it is their constitutional right as part of the pursuit of happiness.

But this raging materialism has left many, many people spiritually impoverished. There is a difference between wanting to improve our financial situation and wanting to be a multimillionaire. The trouble begins when money is worshiped above all things or is used as a way to fill a void in your life that never can be satisfied.

Harold Kushner used a simple little fairy tale by Shel Silverstein to make a profound point. The fairy tale is about a circle that was missing a piece. A large triangular wedge had been cut out of it. The circle wanted to be whole, with nothing missing, so it went around looking for its missing piece. But because it was incomplete, it could only roll very slowly as it rolled through the world. And as it rolled slowly, it admired the flowers along the way. It chatted with butterflies. It was warmed by the sunshine.

The circle found lots of pieces, but none of them fit. Some were too big and some were too small. Some too square, some too pointy. So it left them all by the side of the road and kept on searching. Then one day it found a piece that fit perfectly. It was so happy. Now it could be whole with nothing missing.

The circle incorporated the missing piece into itself and began to roll once again. But now that it was a perfect circle, so it could roll very fast, too fast to notice the flowers and to talk to the butterflies. When the circle realized how different the world seemed when it rolled through it so quickly, it stopped and left the missing piece by the side of the road. It rolled slowly away, once again, looking for its missing piece.

Kushner concludes, "The lesson is that in some strange

sense, we are more whole when we are incomplete—when we are missing something. There is a wholeness about the person who has come to terms with his limitations, who knows what he can and cannot do, the person who is brave enough to let go of his unrealistic dreams and not feel like a failure for doing so."

In the book of Genesis, it says that God brought man and woman into paradise. They lacked nothing inwardly or outwardly because they knew God had given them everything they needed. They felt no hunger, sadness, or loneliness. It was only when they became dissatisfied with what God had given them that they felt an inner void, an emptiness that resulted in their going against God's wishes and their banishment from Eden.

Like succumbing to the temptation of the serpent, the desire for money can get us into deep trouble. Do we spend enough time cultivating a life outside of the material world? Has cash become a replacement for God in our lives? It's understandable how money can become God-like for many people. After all, money has real power. Money can educate us, makes us safer, healthier, and it can even save our lives on occasion. All of this makes money an excellent false god—an idol of sorts because it possesses some of the power the ancients ascribed to God. Money worship also makes what we acquire with money take on an almost existential, holy meaning for many people. We start to believe that these things we purchase and own, the trappings of success, the outer shell we present to the world, are in fact what constitutes our very being. In other words, as philosopher Jacob Needleman put it,

"Our outer life becomes our inner life." When that happens, we are headed for trouble.

It is difficult to achieve a sense of wholeness in a world that ascribes God-like attributes to products. Given the barrage of marketing to make us buy, buy, buy, it's easy to see how money and material goods become our idols. Consider the following slogans from advertisements, and insert the word "God" for the product that is being promoted:

"Don't leave home without it [God]"

"General Foods International Coffees—It [God] stirs the soul."

"Shiseido [God]. I am your . . . strength. Rely on me."

"Ford [God], a better idea."

"You're in good hands with Allstate [God]."

What has happened in this age of marketing is that products, like money, have become the false idols that we worship. As the ad says, we get our *strength* from the things that we buy. We *rely* on these things (cars, houses, cosmetics, or clothes) to lift us up spiritually. When you feel depressed, if you've had a bad day at work, or if you have had an argument with a loved one, do you go on a shopping spree to make yourself feel better? While this may divert your attention for a while, the pleasure that you get from the accumulation of material goods does not last for long. It is not wrong to want to buy nice things, but products will never solve your problems or bring you true contentment.

Likewise, money cannot bring us joy because joy comes from having a balanced life filled with spiritual, as well as material, satisfaction. The Hebrew word *shalom*, which is used to say "hello," "good-bye," and "peace," actually means "wholeness." It means being able to embrace as well as to let go. This is essential to becoming whole. Money is nice, but balance and wholeness should be our goal.

As clichéd as it may sound, material pleasures cannot guarantee personal satisfaction. Anyone who thinks it can is in for a lifetime of disappointment. Believing money or materialism can sustain our souls is not, as philosopher Jacob Needleman points out, a sin. It's a mistake. Like trying to eat a picture of food. The truth, which seems equally facile but is difficult to achieve, is that we all should have as rich an inner life as we do an outer life because things will never afford us a rich inner life. Things are imposters of happiness and meaning.

I'm not suggesting that we give up all our worldly possessions in order to find spiritual integrity. At the same time, we do not have to give up our spiritual foundation in order to find financial success. The desire to be prosperous is not a sin, or even a character flaw. As I said, money is neither good nor bad. It's what we do with it that counts.

When Moses, the man who led the slaves to freedom, went away for forty days without food or water, people were gripped with fear and confusion. They turned to Moses' brother Aaron, asking him to create another leader. Six hundred thousand frightened people shouted, "Make us a god who will go before us." They ripped the gold earrings from their ears and Aaron cast them into the shape of a calf. A dizzying dance of ecstasy began around the golden god.

"This is your god, O Israel, who brought you out of Egypt," the people shouted with reckless conviction. Lost and leaderless, hounded by doubt and fear, these people groped in the spiritual darkness toward a pathetic, little lump of gold.

When Moses finally returned, he discovered that the same people who witnessed God's power while crossing the Red Sea to safety had suddenly given up on God. For their lack of faith, Moses ground the golden calf into dust, cast it upon the water, and forced the people to drink their own debauchery. Then, three thousand of them were killed in a murderous plague of punishment.

Not much later in the Bible, these same people contributed their gold jewelry once again. But this time it was not to fashion a golden calf, but to decorate a tabernacle, a kind of portable sanctuary wherein they could worship God. This act and the place ultimately led the people to a true sense of their religious faith. It's not gold that is evil; it's how we use it. Money today, like gold for our ancestors, is neutral, neither good nor bad. Life is ultimately not about how vast our resources may be, but about how we put our resources—financial, emotional, and spiritual—to use.

Here's a wonderful example of what I mean. Every week for several years, a mild-mannered clerk who worked at a cemetery received an envelope with a money order and a note instructing him to put fresh flowers on a grave.

One day, a car drove up to the cemetery gates, and a

chauffeur came into the clerk's office to speak to him. "The lady outside is too ill to walk," the driver explained. "Would you mind coming with me to speak to her?"

The shy clerk walked over and looked into the car, where a frail, elderly woman with sad eyes sat in the back seat, a bundle of flowers in her arms. "I am Mrs. Adams," the woman said. "I am the one who has been sending you the money orders for the flowers. I came here today myself because the doctors have told me I have only a few weeks left to live. I'm not sorry really. I have nothing left to live for. But before I die, I wanted to take one last look at my son's grave and put the flowers there myself."

"You know, ma'am, I always was sorry you kept sending the money for the flowers," the clerk told her.

"Sorry?"

"Yes, because flowers last such a short time, and no one ever gets to see them. There are thousands of people in hospitals and nursing homes who would love to see and smell fresh flowers. But there isn't anybody at that grave. Not really."

The old woman sat for a while and left without a word. The clerk was afraid he had offended her. But a few months later, he was surprised with another visit. This time there was no chauffeur. The woman had driven herself to the cemetery.

She went to the clerk's office and said, "I've been taking the flowers to people in hospitals and nursing homes, as you suggested. You were right. It does make them happy. And it makes me happy. The doctors don't understand what's making me well, but I do."

It's a simple, true story about the same woman using

the same money to buy the same flowers for two different purposes. Money itself is neutral—neither good nor bad. How we use it makes all the difference in the world.

Net Worth and Self-Worth

Consider what we Americans already have today. David Brooks, author of *Bobos in Paradise*, wrote that the average U.S. household makes $42,000 a year. Factor in a college degree for the major wage earner, and this figure increases to $71,400. A professional degree can push it up even further to more than $100,000. If you are among the college educated who earn approximately $75,000, this means you are richer than 95 percent of the people in the world. Even our poorer citizens live at a higher standard than most of the world, with TVs and VCRs in nearly every home.

And yet, Americans are obsessed with making more because they believe their happiness will increase along with their net worth. Economists who have studied this question found that money only buys us a temporary uptick of happiness. According to one survey conducted by British economist Andrew Oswald, people who came into large amounts of cash unexpectedly reported higher mental well-being during the following year. Their happiness, however, appeared to fade over time. In another study, Oswald found that people with rising incomes became less happy if other people's incomes increased even more.

"Equality reduces happiness," Oswald told a reporter from the *Wall Street Journal*. "So society as a whole might be getting wealthier, but it won't translate into happiness for many unless they are becoming wealthier faster than everybody else." Unfortunately, the urge to stay one step ahead of the Joneses seems a sad part of human nature and one that ultimately leads to nowhere.

For some who are not wealthy, it helps to believe that "have-nots" are morally superior. As Albert Camus said, "It's a kind of spiritual snobbery that makes people think they can be happy without money." Celebrity magazines and gossip columns are filled with stories about the rich and famous who are going through their third or fourth divorce or are in drug rehab, psychiatric hospitals, or jail. People who revel in these stories are filled with what the Germans call *schadenfreude*, which means deriving pleasure from hearing about the misfortune of others.

Tabloid stories like these confirm our belief that we may not have fame or fortune, but at least we're not miserable—that when you strip away all the glitz and glitter, the rich must *really* be unhappy. It helps us get through the struggles of our day. The truth is, some wealthy people are happy, and some are not. The same is true, of course, for those who are not rich.

Is it wrong to harbor these feelings? Right or wrong, it's unproductive. We tend to gossip about people of equal or higher social standing because there is a certain status given to those who are plugged into powerful people. But it's a false perception because people who gossip and obsess about the rich are merely straining at the velvet ropes while the high and mighty pass them by. We will never be satisfied with what we have as long as we compare the size of our net worth like teenaged boys comparing the size of their genitals in a locker room. With the exception of the wealthiest person in the world, there will always be someone who is richer.

So how do we curb this desire to equate our self-worth with our net worth? Money does have real power. It can make us more comfortable. It can buy us a better education, but it can't make us better or wiser people. Only a rich inner life can do that. Part of cultivating a rich inner life is knowing where not to be and who not to be around. This includes, of course, hanging around people who define themselves by money.

When I'm performing a bar mitzvah, for example, I tend to skip the extravagant parties afterward. I don't go to the receptions because I am often uncomfortable with the values that are being represented. By not going, I don't put myself in a position where I either will feel disgusted by or covetous of someone's lifestyle. An alcoholic should stay away from bars, and someone who suffers from money lust or wants to cultivate a rich inner life should stay away from people who are crassly materialistic. It's just that simple.

There have been times in my life when I didn't have much money. My wife and I didn't go out to big fancy dinners; we stayed home and cooked instead. We went for bike rides. We walked the baby around in the stroller and went out for ice cream. Life was simple and good.

More than seven centuries ago, the philosopher Maimonides made a simple and important observation about God and nature. The more something is truly needed by human beings, he observed, the more abundant it is in nature. For example, we need air most of all, then water, then basic food. Air, water, and basic foodstuffs like grains, fruits, and vegetables are exactly what are most common and affordable. The less something is truly necessary, the rarer it will be in nature. And yet, as Maimonides points out, these rare things are the things people often spend their time and money seeking. People haven't changed much in seven centuries. Many of us still chase after the rare, expensive, and unnecessary. Many of us still confuse what we want with what we need, and many of us fail to realize just how abundant nature really is in meeting those needs.

The great rabbi and philosopher Abraham Joshua Heschel said, "To have more is not to be more," and William James, the psychologist who originated the idea of pragmatism, said, "Lives based on having are less free than lives based either on doing or being." This is why the Jewish tradition of not handling money during the Sabbath can be so liberating. Many who observe the Sabbath in this way say it is their favorite day of the week. You walk, talk, visit friends, and eat together. You can't spend money, so you are forced to form stronger relationships. The Sabbath is the day when each of us can declare an armistice in the battle to have more.

"It is physically impossible," said the nineteenth-century historian John Ruskin, "for a well-educated, intellectual, or brave man to make money the chief object of his thoughts; just as it is for him to make his dinner the principal object of them. All healthy people like their dinners, but their dinner is not the main object of their lives. So all healthily minded people like making money, ought to like it, and to enjoy the sensation of winning it; but the main object of their life is not money; it is something better than money." For Ruskin, as it ought to be for us, the pursuit of money is a matter of degree, of balance and of clarity about what money is for and what it can or cannot do.

When I ask them about how much is enough, nearly every wealthy person I know tells me that the answer has changed as their wealth has increased. "I thought at one time that if I had a million dollars in the bank I would really be secure," one television producer told me. "But after that first million was put away, I felt that I needed more because as my income increased, so did my expenses. The more I make, the more I spend, the more I spend, the more I need to make. At this point, I am honest enough about myself to say that I will never feel like enough is enough."

It's hard to feel sorry for someone as wealthy as this man is, but I do. Golden handcuffs are still handcuffs.

Consider King Solomon and the story of three brothers who came to him and asked: "How can we become as wise as you are? May we stay here and serve you and learn?"

The king agreed, but only on the condition that they stay for three years. The brothers accepted. They sat by the king whenever he decided the many cases brought to him, and they watched him discuss complex ideas with other learned men.

A few years passed, but the brothers felt they had not grown any wiser. They said to the king: "Your Majesty, we have decided to return home to our wives because our stay here has not profited us at all."

"Very well," replied the king. "In that case, I release you from my service. Because you are leaving, I will offer each of you one hundred gold coins or three wise sayings. Which shall it be?"

The king waited as each brother considered the choice. They decided to take the gold coins. As they rode away from the palace, the youngest brother suddenly regretted his choice and said, "Brothers, I must return to King Solomon. I don't want the gold. I would rather have the wisdom he offered. Come, let us return to the palace to ask for his wise words. What else did we work and hope for all these years?"

But the brothers insisted that they continue on their way home. "Give up one hundred gold coins for three wise sayings?" they scoffed. "Give us your gold, and we'll tell you three sayings!" they laughed mockingly as they rode off.

The youngest brother returned to the palace and was brought before the king. "I came here to gain wisdom and not gold. I regret that I did not accept your wise sayings in the first place. Please take back the coins you have given me, and give me your good counsel instead."

The king was delighted by his request, and said, "Here are the three sayings for you to heed: when you travel, journey only by daylight, and find your place to sleep before darkness falls; when you find a river swollen with water, wait and do not cross; when you meet your wife, confide in her as a friend."

The youngest brother thanked King Solomon and sped off to catch up with his brothers. But when they met again, the youngest brother said nothing about what

Solomon had told him. The three rode along until they came to an inn. Although it was still daylight, the youngest brother, remembering Solomon's advice, said, "Let's remain here for the night."

The brothers protested, saying, "It will still be light for several more hours. Why waste the time when we could be traveling farther. Is this the kind of wise advice you received from Solomon? Stay here if you wish, but we will continue on our journey."

The youngest brother stayed at the inn and, when darkness fell, he was warm and comfortable. He ate a good dinner, and his horse was cared for and had plenty to eat and drink as well.

Meanwhile, the two brothers who had continued up the mountain got caught in a snowstorm. They became trapped among the ice-covered rocks and froze to death.

At dawn the next day, the youngest brother set out on his journey home. When he reached the mountain pass, he discovered his two brothers' frozen bodies and wept. He buried them as best he could in the frozen ground, taking the gold they had received from the king.

When he reached the other side of the mountain, he saw a river in the distance. It was overflowing with water that rushed and swirled along the banks. Remembering, once again, the words of Solomon, the youngest brother decided to remain on high ground until the waters receded. As he looked down, he saw two men driving several heavily laden mules toward the river. "Wait! Don't cross! It's dangerous," he shouted down to the men struggling against the swollen waters. But they ignored his cries, and soon the men and beasts were drowned.

When the waters returned to their usual level, the youngest brother began to cross. On the way, he found the drowned animals with bags of gold, and he took the gold with him.

When he finally returned home, wealthy and in good health, he embraced his wife. Now, for the third time, he recalled Solomon's advice. He told his wife everything that had happened to him and to his brothers. The brothers' wives came to greet him, and they were distraught to hear about the death of their husbands. Seeing the bags of gold, they shouted, "You murdered them for the gold! That gold belongs to us! We will take you to court, and you shall be tried and hanged."

The family went to the King Solomon, knowing that he would settle the dispute fairly. When Solomon heard the case, he recognized the youngest brother and confirmed his story. He returned the gold he had given the other brothers to their wives, but said: "Remember, always seek wisdom, for wisdom is more precious than gold."

An Attitude of Gratitude

Comparing ourselves to others is an unavoidable part of human nature. It's not always easy to be happy with what we have. But we all need to incorporate more gratitude into our lives. Some of us remind ourselves by going to church or synagogue that we should be grateful for the riches in our life: our family, friends, work, and daily bread. Sadly, this feeling of gratitude often evaporates as soon as we return to our everyday lives. We move quickly from grateful to resentful, consumed by petty jealousies, old grudges, and our real or imagined needs.

Perhaps we are a bit like the Hebrew slaves whom Moses led to freedom through the parting seas. After crossing the sea, the people wandered through the desert, where God brought water forth from the rocks and manna fell from heaven like dancing snowflakes. The people gathered, then ground and cooked the seed-like substance into cakes that the Bible tells us tasted like "rich cream." You would think that after four hundred years of oppression this manna from heaven would have made them happy.

But what did these former slaves do in response to their good fortune? They complained. They whined to God that they had "nothing but this manna." They complained as if to say, "We are bored, God. We want a little excitement. A little variety." They were people who had everything, but saw themselves as having nothing.

How many of us have said, "I *need* a new car" or "I *need* a new dress"? How often do we really need what we want? What we really need is to remind ourselves on a daily basis how fortunate we are and how grateful we ought to be. I know that there are some people who don't have much to be grateful for monetarily. There are many poor people in the world who genuinely *need*. Are you one of them?

The Chassidic rabbi and singer Shlomo Carlbach put it nicely when he said: "You know, when you have no money and you really need a cup of coffee, you pray, 'God, please give me a quarter for a cup of coffee. I'm really at the end.' But when you have a thousand dollars, you don't remember to pray for a quarter. What's so special is when you have the money and you still remember to ask God to give. There was a holy rabbi who, even when the food was on the table in front of him, before he'd eat it, he'd pray, 'Please, God, feed me.'"

Whenever I forget how fortunate I am, some member of my congregation who is in need reminds me. Here's just one week's worth of calls. There's Robert, who calls to tell me that he is starting radiation and chemotherapy for a tumor lodged in his brain. Even if he beats it, the experts say the tumor will be back in one to five years. It's a lot for a twenty-five-year-old to take.

Melissa calls to see me. She's forty-four, bright, attractive, wildly successful, and alone. She longs for a man with whom she can share her life, for children, for deep, abiding, human love. "Have you found anyone to fix me up with yet?" she asks hopefully.

Amy calls to tell me that she lost her job. There wasn't enough business to keep her. She's living on unemployment and worried about losing her apartment. Do I know anyone who might be able to help?

David calls. "Rabbi," he trembles through his tears, "yesterday my wife told me she's leaving. What's going to happen to our twenty-month-old son, to me, to my life? Please, will you talk to her, Rabbi?"

The same day, I get a call from the principal of my son's school. One of the families which has a son in my son's class lost their two-year-old the night before. He was acting a little lethargic during the day. Then, in the early evening, while they were holding him in their arms, he suddenly stiffened and died. No one knows why. "They're a Jewish family with no temple," the principal tells me. "Their hearts are broken. Could you step in and help them?"

We all long for bigger, better, and more. But we take so much for granted. How desperately all the people with whom I talked within that single week hungered for the manna of work, family, health, life, or love, for the simple good fortune that pours like rich cream upon most of us each day. For this, we should be grateful.

CHAPTER TWO | # Eye of the Needle

"WE MAKE A LIVING BY WHAT
WE GET. WE MAKE A LIFE BY WHAT
WE GIVE."

—UNKNOWN

‖ Both the Hebrew and the Christian bibles make numerous references to wealth, debt, and poverty. In fact, if you cut out every reference to the poor and needy in the Bible, it would be ripped to shreds. The Hebrew Bible, which contains holy writings for both Jews and Christians, is obsessed with three things: the battle against idolatry, the perpetuation of the Israelite people, and, most predominantly, the way we treat the widow, stranger, and orphan.

Why does the Bible command us to reach out to the powerless? Because, "We too were strangers in the land of Egypt." Because our ancestors knew what it meant to be powerless, we have an obligation to help the disenfranchised of today. Although the Bible would never put it this way, once we arrive at the upper levels of wealth and privilege, we have to send the elevator back down for others. We must always remember that the reason we have power, if we are lucky enough to possess it, is because we stand on the shoulders of the shoulders of the shoulders of those who came before us.

Time and time again, the Bible commands us to be grateful for what we have and to help the poor. According to ancient tradition, each Israelite family was originally given an equal share of land provided to them by God. In theory, at least, everyone originally had an equal slice of the prosperity pie.

Every fifty years, a "Jubilee year" was proclaimed, wherein those who had lost their land through financial misfortune had it returned to them. Every seventh year, a "Sabbatical year" was designated as a year in which the remaining portion of unpaid debts was nullified and slaves were set free. Theoretically, in biblical society, no one could remain very poor, or very rich, for very long.

Do historians believe this system was strictly adhered to? No. Was the chasm between rich and poor as wide then as it is now? Probably. But what the Bible set out to do was to create an ideal toward which we should strive. And ideal that would put an end to systemic, multigenerational poverty.

The Hebrew Bible does not speak so much about money as it does about wealth. In ancient times, wealth was measured by the size of one's herd and the number of one's wives and children. It was an agrarian, patriarchal society. Those who owned land were not allowed to harvest the corners of the field—those parts that were missed when the plow turned around. Farmers were expected to set aside this part of the field for the widow, stranger, and orphan.

Money was originally created as a way of temporarily transferring wealth to assist those in need. In fact, one of the early Hebrew words for money is *zuz*, which comes from the verb *lazuz*, meaning to circulate. So the point of money was not to be amassed or hoarded, but to be circulated in the community to uplift the poor. Money was merely a vehicle by which our ancestors created a more fair society.

Money and poverty are central topics in the Christian Bible as well. Christ's attitude toward money was fairly negative, at least by our modern standards. He saw it as an entrapment that prevented us from focusing our ideas on God. He said, for example, "It's easier for a camel to go through the eye of a needle than it is for a rich man to enter the Kingdom of Heaven." The disciples, who were bemused by this statement, asked Jesus, "Then who can be saved?" Christ responded by saying, "With God all things are possible."

In another biblical passage, a rich, young ruler comes to Jesus and says, "What do I do to enter the Kingdom of Heaven?" Jesus answers, "Sell all you have to give to the poor." The ruler goes away sorrowful because he is unwilling to do this. So how do Christians make sense of Christ's view that money and possessions get in the way of our relationship with God?

My friend, Reverend Kirk Smith, a minister at Saint James Episcopal Church in Los Angeles, says the church does not expect that people live up to Christ's model of absolute poverty, although, he says, it is an ideal to which many have returned throughout Christian history. He cited St. Francis of Assisi, who literally shed everything, including the clothes on his back, as one of the most dramatic examples of that ideal. St. Francis earned all of what he needed by begging, and his followers also were expected to rid themselves of their possessions.

In the early days of Christianity, the church called on its followers to practice what amounted to a communal system of living, where everything was shared. The idea, similar to that in the Hebrew Bible, was that it's okay to have property, but one must share so that no one is in need and so no one is accumulating riches exclusively for himself or herself. This philosophy is quite strong in the Christian Bible. In one passage, a couple offers the Apostle Peter some of their possessions. Peter knew, however, that they were holding back on what they were giving. He asked, "Is this everything you have?" When the couple said it was, they were struck down dead.

While Peter's expectations of the couple were unrealistic by most standards, the Bible often exaggerates to make a point. Nevertheless, the point is a simple and profound one. We only truly receive in the deepest sense of the word when we give. The less selfish we are, not only with our money but also with our time, our hearts, and our souls, the richer we become.

The Gospel of Wealth

In his essay, "The Gospel of Wealth," written in 1889, steel magnate and philanthropist Andrew Carnegie had this to say about the duty of a wealthy person:

> First, to set an example of modest, unostentatious living, shunning display or extravagance; to provide moderately for the legitimate wants of those dependent upon him; and, after doing so, to consider all surplus revenues which come to him simply as trust funds, which he is called upon to administer, and strictly bound as a matter of duty

to administer in the manner which, in his judgment is best calculated to produce the most benefi-
cial results for the community—the man of wealth
thus becoming the mere trustee and agent for his
poorer brethren, bringing to their service his superior wisdom, experience, and ability to administer,
doing for them better than they would or could do
for themselves. . . .

The day is not far distant when the man who dies
leaving behind him millions of available wealth,
which was free for him to administer during life,
will pass away 'unwept, unhonored, and unsung,'
no matter to what uses he leaves the dross which he
cannot take with him. Of such as these the public
verdict will then be: 'The man who dies thus rich
dies disgraced.' Such, in my opinion, is the true
gospel concerning wealth, obedience to which is
destined some day to solve the problem of the rich
and the poor.

Carnegie took the Bible's teachings seriously, and the
Bible implores us to "reach out to the orphan, widow,
and the stranger. Feed and clothe them." But it seems
harder and harder to get people to reach out and care
these days.

Up to the time of Reformation, poverty was considered a good thing by the faithful. Even people who had
money looked at being poor as a way to get into heaven.
But attitudes toward the poor began to change as people
parted with the Roman Catholic Church. The rising middle class in Europe found the Protestant view toward

money far more congenial. John Calvin, one of the six-teenth-century reformers, preached the doctrine of predestination. Calvin believed that God knew from the beginning of creation who would be saved and who would be damned, and there was nothing anyone could do to change things.

How did you know if you were saved? Calvinists believed that those who were successful, God-fearing, hard-working citizens were destined for salvation, and that the poor were shiftless, lazy, and got what they deserved. Of course, this idea has become divorced from its religious roots, but it was the basis of what we now call the Protestant work ethic.

Of course, the problem with this so-called Protestant work ethic and Calvin's notion of predestination is that most of the world's poor are not people who can simply work their way out of poverty. Some people are poor because they are lazy, but most of the world's poor—and certainly most of America's poor—are elderly or children.

Where does this leave Jews and Christians today? We all must wrestle with the problem of how to use our money properly. Both Jews and Christians believe that everything we have, including our possessions, health, and relationships, is a gift from God. It is all on loan to us, and we can't take it with us after we leave this Earth.

Unfortunately, many of us have not fully embraced our obligation to help the poor. For Christians, it's the idea of stewardship, and for Jews, it's called *tzedaka*. *Tzedaka*, which is commonly translated as "charity," really comes from the word "justice." So the idea of giving money to help the poor is not seen as charitable or nice, but as something that is the *right* or *just* thing to do. Similarly, many think the Hebrew word *mitzvah* means "good deed," but it actually means "commandment." Helping the poor isn't just a good deed. It's a requirement.

We all know that we receive when we give. We receive in the larger sense by creating a more equitable society and in the smaller, personal sense as well. But regardless of whether or not we receive pleasure or credit by giving, giving to those in need is a sacred obligation, not an option. Period.

The disciple Luke expressed our obligation to the poor by saying, "From everyone to whom much has been given, much will be required; and from one to whom much has been entrusted, even more will be expected." While the television producer felt that the more he had the more he needed to make, the Bible's view is that the more we have, the more we are expected to give. John Wesley, founder of the Methodist Church, reiterated this credo by saying, "Work as hard as you can, to earn as much as you can, to give away as much as you can."

Even if we don't give until in hurts, we can start by tithing, which calls for giving 10 percent of our adjusted gross earnings to those in need. This does not mean taking a vow of poverty like St. Francis in order to please God. It's 10 percent—not 100 percent. As Jerold Mundis wrote in his book *Making Peace with Money:*

> Generosity is a quality of unselfishness, not self-sacrifice. Self-sacrifice is voluntarily accepting—or even inflicting upon oneself—pain so that someone else may benefit: a mother going without in order

to feed her children, a lover stepping in to absorb a blow meant for a beloved, a soldier throwing himself on a hand grenade to save his fellow. Unselfishness, on the other hand, is simply being openhanded, the opposite of fearful, covetous, and grasping.

Practicing generosity helps overcome a siege mentality, a belief that there isn't enough for us, and that we must defend what little we have. It relaxes the spirit, provides a sense of well-being, and facilitates the flow of money into and through a life. Ultimately, it makes your world a better place to live.

When it comes down to it, generosity is not only an unselfish act, it's a matter of commitment. The idea of commitment is a hard one for some people to grasp, as in this joke about one of the wealthiest men in the country. It was widely known that this particular man had never given anything to charity, despite his enormous wealth. One day, an organization that helps the needy contacted him for a contribution.

"We've been checking up on you, Mr. Goldsworth," the fundraiser says. "Not only do you own a mansion in Beverly Hills, but you have another home in Palm Springs, as well as a chalet in Switzerland. You drive a Rolls, your wife owns a Mercedes, and you recently opened up a dozen new offices. Mr. Goldsworth, would you be willing to make a commitment to our charity?"

Goldsworth listened quietly, with arms resolutely folded around his considerable girth. "Commitment?" he asked. "I'll tell you about commitment. My sister's paraplegic son has $125,000 a year in medical bills. My grandson is learning disabled and has to attend a special school that costs $25,000 a year. And my mother has Alzheimer's and needs round-the-clock care that costs $50,000 a year. Commitment? I'll tell you about commitment. If I can say no to them, I can say no to you!"

We laugh, but the truth is there's a little Goldsworth in each of us. We all want to hide from the world's problems. It's hard to part with what we have to help those who have less. We work hard. We've got bills and expenses. But while we are hiding and hoarding, nearly forty-two thousand children in the world die of hunger and malnutrition every day. How can we turn our backs on children?

THE INVISIBLE POOR

Many years ago in a small Russian village there lived only one wealthy man. Everyone else in the village suffered terribly through the hot summers and wickedly cold winters with barely enough food to eat and little if any fuel to heat their homes.

During a particularly brutal winter, the priest came to visit the rich man. He knocked on his door as the wind howled. The rich man opened the door in his shirtsleeves while the fire crackled in the background. He immediately invited the priest in.

"How is your lovely wife?" the priest asked the man, while he still stood in his doorway.

"She's fine, thank you. Why don't you come in?"

"And your brother in Kiev, is he well also?"

"Yes, yes," the rich man answered. "Come inside and we'll talk."

"You have a son studying in Moscow, do you not?" asked the priest.

"I do," answered the man, beginning to shiver in his own doorway. "Now, come inside."

"I can't come inside," the priest responded. "You see, I have come to ask you for money to buy fuel so that the poor can heat their homes. But if I come inside, you and I will sit by the warm fire, and you won't understand. If, on the other hand, we stand here in the doorway and you shiver, then you will understand better why the poor need your help."

With that, the rich man agreed and gave the priest enough money to keep the villagers warm.

Here's a story that makes people laugh whenever I tell it. But the more we think about it, the less funny it becomes. It's a story about a minister who was three hours late coming home one evening. As each hour passed, his wife became angrier, until he finally walked in the door. "Where have you been?" she asked her husband. "You said you would be home hours ago."

"I was at a meeting trying to convince the rich to give to the poor," the pastor said, exhausted. Feeling more sympathetic, his wife then asked softly, "And were you successful?"

"I was half successful," the minister answered. "So far, the poor have agreed to accept!"

It's a good story. But there's a certain sadness to it as well. Of course the poor are ready to accept. But are we prepared to give? It's hard to cut away what the Bible calls "the thickening of our hearts." This "thickening" comes in part, I think, because most of us see and hear so little of the poor. Most of us live middle-class lives or better in middle-class neighborhoods or better. The poor are often far from sight or neatly dressed in uniforms as they wait on our tables, cut our grass, or wash our cars. It's hard to remember the poor when we do not really live among them.

A friend of mine who advocates for the disabled in Washington, D.C. called to tell me about a friend of his who lives in a gated Florida community with tremendous mansions. Apparently, there is one particular street where the houses are even more spectacular than the others in the community are. So grandiose, in fact, that the residents of the gated community would often drive down this specific street just to gawk at the houses.

So what do you think the owners of the big mansions decided to do? They decided to gate their street as well. Now, there is gated street inside the gated community! It's an extreme example of a common problem. Those of us who are not poor are isolated from those who are. That isolation makes it easy to forget about the poor.

Aggie Max is a welfare mother living on the streets, and her story, published in an online magazine *Salon.com*, touched me deeply. She calls it, "The Bag Lady and the Banquet."

I always pass by a house in the park between the lakeshore drive and the water, across from the main public library, called the Edgemere House. Once the private residence of a wealthy family, it is now a landmark belonging to the city and free guided tours are shown through it on certain days. It can also be reserved for private parties, wedding receptions, and such. . . .

Today as I pass the house I notice that it is set up for some sort of event, with tables on the back lawn and a multitude of white flowers and ribbons. A wedding party, I assume. . . .

Perhaps a hundred people dressed in gowns and tuxedos . . . wander in and out of the house chattering gaily, holding drinks, laughing, and sparkling. Two of them (which two I couldn't figure out) had just been married. . . .

A chamber music ensemble with recorders and flutes replaces the string quartet, which has been playing on the glassed-in sun porch, and the music is exquisite, lovely. . . .

The people at the tables are being served by uniformed waiters and waitresses. (A waitress stands outside the service entrance, smoking. A wino approaches her and asks her for a cigarette. She gives him one. She lights it for him.) . . .

After a while I move a little closer to the fence. The guests are all talking loudly, perhaps unnecessarily so, and I want to listen to the conversations. I think of the image of a zoo; it is They [sic] who are in a cage. . . .

A mild-looking middle-aged woman, sitting at a table near the fence, has attracted my attention. She smiles at me, makes a gesture. I stare back but do not acknowledge. She points at me, then at the table in front of her where there sits a plate containing a large uneaten sandwich. She assumes that I'm hungry. . . . But I'm not; I'm still faintly queasy from lunch at St. Vinnie's.

She sneaks a look around to ascertain that no other wedding guest has observed her gesture. Maybe it's in bad taste to take such liberties with the host's catered food. She doesn't want to be seen giving me the sandwich, but she wants to be able to talk about it later. Or feel good about it later. How much middle class guilt can be appeased by one sandwich? In such a way as not to be observed from within or without, except by me, she eases the plate through the bars and places it on the grass just outside the fence.

She looks at me hungrily, waiting for me to accept her offering. This pisses me off, for some reason, and I turn away. The Deliberate Snub. I conceive the scenario of myself crawling to the food on my hands and knees and cramming it into my mouth like an animal with appropriate slobbering and grunting noises. What I would really like to do is wrap the sonofabitch up and take it "home" for later. But I can't bring myself to do anything. When I turn back to look, the woman is gone but the plate is still there.

A ragged, skeletal, fevered-looking derelict stumbles by.

"Hey, man," I say to this specter. "There's a sandwich over there if you're hungry."

He looks at me, then at the plate. His eyes light up. "Gee, wow, thanks!" he says. He stumbles toward the fence, falls on his knees, and begins to devour the food with grunting, slobbering noises. I get up and walk away, not looking back. . . .

The whole episode allowed me a feeling of small triumph, which lasted about ten minutes, until I stopped to think about this woman who had the kindness to notice the less fortunate stranger outside looking in.

I begin to wonder—what if I were in her position? Would I have shown such generosity of spirit?

I suspect not. I'd probably have turned my back on the whole miserable assortment of dregs and creeps and said . . . "Fuck 'em. They get what they get."

Aggie Max understands. She, homeless and poor, understands that if she weren't homeless and poor, she'd have a hard time reaching out herself. It's hard to reach out, to care, to notice, to share. It's hard to "cut away the thickening of our hearts."

Yet there are so many good and generous people among us, even if we don't realize it. Folk tales abound teaching the virtue of giving. One of my favorites is about a poor shoemaker, who was the most generous man in his village. He responded to every person in need and every charitable cause that was brought to his attention. No one was ever turned away empty-handed from his door.

One day a man in the village known as the Miser died. The village leaders decided to bury him at the edge of the cemetery. No one mourned his passing; no one followed the funeral procession to the place of burial. As the days passed, the rabbi heard disturbing news regarding the shoemaker. "He no longer gives alms to the beggars," complained one man. "He has refused every charity that has approached him," declared another.

"Has anyone asked about his change of heart?" inquired the rabbi.

"Yes," replied the first man. "He says he no longer has money to give away."

So the rabbi decided to call on the shoemaker himself. "Why have you suddenly ceased giving money to worthy causes?" he asked the shoemaker.

Slowly the shoemaker began to speak. "Many years ago, the man you called the Miser came to me with a huge sum of money and asked me to distribute it to beggars and charities. He made me promise that I would not reveal the source of the money until after he died. Once every month, he would visit me secretly and give me additional money to distribute. I became known as a great benefactor even though I never spent a penny of my own money. I am surprised that no one questioned me earlier. Didn't anyone wonder how I, who earned the wages of a cobbler, could afford to give away as much money as I have all these years?"

The rabbi called all of the villagers together and told them the story. "The Miser has lived by the Scriptures, keeping his charity a secret," the rabbi told them. Then they all walked to the grave of the Miser and prayed. When he died, the rabbi asked to be buried near the fence, next to the grave of the man known as the Miser.

This kind of anonymous giving is a humble, pious, meaningful way of helping the poor. But there is an even better way—the way of empowering the poor to use their own talents to succeed. This is far from a new idea. One of my favorite old parables demonstrates giving through empowerment as well as any I know.

As the story goes, a vagrant knocked on a monk's door begging food and a night's shelter. Feeding him, the monk told him he knew of an abandoned cottage where, through God's mercy, the man could stay if he wished. Perhaps he could even dig some roots and pick berries to get himself a little food.

The next morning the monk took the man to the cottage. Its walls were so old and weatherworn that rain could blow through in a dozen places. The roof had fallen in. The chimney was cracked and crumbling. Vines and nettle bushes grew all around the tangled profusion.

"Trust in God to provide what is needed," said the monk, before he left.

The following month, the monk happened to pass by the cottage again and saw that it had a new thatched roof. "God and you have certainly found a way to keep the rain off your head," he said.

"Yes, we have," the man answered gratefully.

The next month, the monk saw that all the walls had been chinked and the window frames set right. "God and you have certainly made a cozy shelter," he said.

"Yes, we have," the man answered gratefully.

The following month, the monk saw that ground had been cleared and the soil tilled for a garden. "God and you are certainly making ready a source of sustenance," the monk said.

"Yes, we are," the man answered gratefully.

So it went for a year. The following summer, the monk marveled at the gleaming cottage with its new chimney and comfortable porch, its freshly dug well from which sweet water could be drawn, its well-tended garden, fruitful with ripening vegetables, and clever hutches stoked with forest rabbits the man had caught. The man himself was busy digging out a root cellar.

"How truly wonderful is all that God and you have done to reclaim this old place!" the monk exclaimed.

The man paused to mop his brow. "Yes," he said. "And you'll remember how hard a time God was having when he had to do it all by himself."

When people hear the phrase, "God will provide," it does not mean that God provides without any effort from humanity. We are meant to be God's partners in repairing the world.

According to the medieval philosopher Maimonides, there is a hierarchy of values when it comes to charity, each one higher than the next:

1. The first and lowest rung on the ladder is to give grudgingly and reluctantly or with regret.
2. The second is to give less than one should, but with grace.
3. The third is to give what one should, but only after being asked.
4. The fourth is to give before one is asked.
5. Number five is to give without knowing who will

receive it; only the recipient knows the identity of the giver.

6. Number six is to give anonymously.

7. Seven is to give so that neither the giver nor the receiver knows the identity of the other.

8. The eighth and highest level of giving is to help someone to become self-supporting by finding employment.

It is interesting that Maimonides believed the greatest form of charity was to help people to help themselves, an idea that fits well into our American ideal of what really works in combating poverty. This approach is clearly the most dignified of all. Something the monk of long ago understood.

Time Is Money

If you think you don't have enough time or money to give, think about Sylvia Orzoff, whom I read about in the *Los Angeles Times* many years ago. Sylvia is a seventy-eight-year-old, ninety-one-pound woman with diabetes and a pacemaker. Six days each week, virtually every week of the year from 8:00 A.M. until noon, rain or shine, well or sick, this tiny, frail, retired waitress stood outside Canter's delicatessen in Los Angeles with a tin blue and white box urging people to donate to the Jewish National Fund.

"Ladies and gentlemen," her plea begins. "You got two dollars? Put one in here. How 'bout it, beautiful?" she says addressing one of the younger customers. "You got money?" she asks a woman half her age in a bright beach dress. The nicely dressed woman puts cash in her box. "Have a good day," Sylvia tells the woman. She turns to the reporter and adds, "I don't like her dress, but I like her money."

It's a routine Sylvia performed without fail for twenty-four years. How much money could little Sylvia have raised with her deli-front entreaties? Hundreds, maybe thousands? Try $2.5 million, most of it in quarters.

Few, if any of us, have the time, the energy, or the determination of Sylvia Orzoff. But that's not really the point. The importance of her story isn't the $2.5 million, as amazing as that may be. It's the way she raised it—one quarter at a time. The significance of Sylvia's example lies not in the greatness of her act, but in its relative smallness. A tiny woman, collecting tiny sums, and inspiring others. When Sylvia retired and moved to the desert, another woman, almost as old as Sylvia, took her place in front of the delicatessen. Even a little bit can add up to a lot. One person, one day, one quarter, one kind and decent act at a time.

The truth is, we could all give more than we do. Think about all the money we spend on celebrations like weddings, bar mitzvahs, birthdays, confirmations, and christenings. These celebrations of life and joy are excellent opportunities to share our good fortune with others. Are we requiring our children to give a percentage of what they receive as gifts to charity? Are we sending uneaten food to a homeless shelter? When my son had his bar mitzvah, we said he could choose the charity, but 10 percent of what he received had to be donated. If he refused, he would be allowed to keep nothing. It was as simple as that.

Remember the biblical story of the tower of Babel? People decided they wanted to build a tower in order to reach God. They enslaved many other people to accomplish the goal. The slaves carried brick after brick after brick to the top of the tower. If someone dropped a brick, the loss of the brick was mourned, but if a worker fell, so be it. Their ideal was to use wealth and power to create an edifice that would make mortals more God-like. In the end, of course, God is displeased by this human endeavor and confounds it by having all the people speak different languages. (This is where the expression to "babble" comes from.) Ultimately, the tower collapses and the bricks are scattered all over the Earth.

What does the story tell us? It tells us that God is displeased when we use our wealth only for our own egos. What pleases God is when we use our means to create a more just, fair, and equitable society.

The Bible says when we give back, God will be "ever present in our midst." The Talmud, a later work of Jewish law, says, "*Tzedaka* averts death." I always was troubled by that phrase. Did the ancient rabbis, who certainly saw many righteous people die, really believe that charity could prevent death? Were they really that naïve? Then I came across a beautiful story that explains what I think the sages were getting at when they claimed, "*Tzedaka* averts death."

A pious man whose wife was dying, turned to his son and said, "Tomorrow is the Sabbath. Be sure to find a needy person to join us for Sabbath dinner." The boy did as his father requested, but he was angry. How could his father think of dinner with the poor at a time like this, with his mother at death's door? But the boy did as he was told. The next day, his mother died.

"Father," the son said, "Yesterday, when you told me to find a poor person to join us for Sabbath dinner, I was angry with you. But then I remembered the verse that says, "*Tzedaka* averts death," and I realized you were just trying to save Mother's life."

"No," the grieving father said to his son. "It's not the lives of people we love or even our own lives that are saved through *tzedaka*. I wasn't preventing the death of your mother. I was preventing the death of God in the world. Being generous and kind averts God's death."

Nearly forty years ago, Lyndon Johnson declared war on poverty. But today, we are still fighting that same war. And in the middle of all the rhetoric, we sometimes lose sight of the facts:

- One in five children under eighteen years old in the United States is poor.
- Every thirty-five seconds an infant is born into poverty in the United States.
- Children are the poorest age group and are twice as likely to be poor as elderly people.
- Five million children go to bed hungry each night in America.

These are unthinkable statistics, especially for the richest country in the world. There is no shortage of people who need our help. Fortunately, there is no shortage of ways to give money and time to the poor. If you are blessed with good fortune, you can give 10 percent of what you earn to those who are needy. Or you can do what Sylvia Orzoff did and give a percentage of your time. You can invite people to sup at your table, like the pious man whose wife lay dying, or simply, like the woman at the wedding—reach out and offer a helping hand.

Chapter Three

For Richer and for Poorer

"When you marry for money, you pay for everything you get."

—Jacob Marcus

‖ I ASKED MY WIFE, BETSY, TO marry me on our second date. We were in our twenties, and Betsy had all of four hundred dollars in her bank account. I was a graduate student making a whopping eleven thousand dollars per year running a Sunday school. My parents were paying for my tuition, so I was doing okay at the time.

Because I was the big breadwinner, I'd pick up the check whenever we went out for dinner. I remember Betsy saying, "It really bothers me that right now I can't contribute anything financially to this marriage." I just looked at her and said, "Honey, we're in this together. I don't keep track of who pays what. Whatever I make is for the both of us from here on in." This is the way we dealt with merging our lives and resources, but everyone is different when it comes to money and marriage.

As a rabbi, I've counseled many couples before, during, and, unfortunately, after wedlock. They come to me with myriad issues, including conflicts about money. This is not surprising because sociologists have found that money is the number one cause of divorce—over sex, kids, and infidelity.

There's no question that money can change a relationship, be it a marriage, a dating couple, or a friendship. But understand that money in any relationship is never simply about money: it's about power. It's about the power that money gives you in terms of status and the power that you give money through your fears, expectations, and past experiences. I view money in the same way that I see other challenges in a marriage, such as sex, raising children, in-laws, or work.

Like these other issues, money can give you an opportunity to create a shared vision for your life together. It can allow you to work as a team, rather than as self-interested individuals. It can also cause tremendous pain, if you let it. Rich or poor, the challenge is the same. It's not about how much or how little you have, but how lovingly and sensitively you approach this issue to achieve your shared values.

One of the most common money disputes in a relationship arises when a spender hooks up with a saver. And unlike Lucy and Ricky Ricardo, it's not the least bit funny. What do you do when two different money philosophies are in a head-on collision?

When engaged couples come to see me, I tell them there are six people in every marriage: your parents, your spouse's parents, and you. What I mean by this is that all of your past comes into play when you are planning to spend your life together. The way you handle money today comes directly from the values you've been taught by your parents.

If you grew up in a penny-pinching family, for example, you might feel that it is unseemly to spend money frivolously. Perhaps your parents had to work long hours and assuaged their guilt with material things. Problems arise when we unwittingly repeat the dysfunctional messages about money that we were taught in our childhood. Even if your childhood wasn't dysfunctional, you might find that your views on money, savings, and investing are incompatible.

This is why every couple must have a money discussion *before* they are married, however distasteful it might seem. What are your earliest associations concerning money? Who paid the bills in your family? Did both parents work? What did your parents do about allowances? Did your parents get divorced and fight about child support?

Money discussions can be an excellent way to learn about what's going on in your relationship. It's an opportunity to start thinking about your similarities and differences, your dreams and fears, and how you can work together to make the sum greater than the parts. It all comes down to teamwork and the willingness to get help both financially and spiritually, if you need it.

MONEY MUSCLE

Money is really about power. So if one partner makes more than the other does, then a power struggle inevitably ensues. Although the two-paycheck household is increasingly the norm in this country, when children arrive, it is often the woman who stays home with the kids or takes the lower-paying job. The financial imbalance this creates might cause the husband to say, "I make the money, so I make the decisions."

This kind of thinking is infantilizing for the spouse without earnings because, like a child, she has to go to daddy for her allowance to buy even the most basic necessities. It's no wonder that this is one of the issues that sparked the feminist movement. Both partners must understand that raising children is work—perhaps the most important job of all. In a perfect world, the one who is giving up a career to be with the children should be compensated proportionally for lost wages. Sadly, as Adam and Eve discovered, this is not a perfect world. Instead, sit down together and figure out how much money the home worker needs on a monthly basis for both household expenses and discretionary income.

Conversely, if a woman has more money than her husband does, he can feel emasculated. Our society still measures a man by the size of his wallet, so it takes a strong ego to accept a relationship where the wife is making top dollar. Such is the case for Cynthia, an actress who inherited tens of millions of dollars from her grandfather. Cynthia recently married Prentice, who was comfortable, but still needed to work for a living. Cynthia confessed that the disparity in their finances was starting to tarnish the relationship.

"I wish I knew why money has a corrupting influence, but it does," Cynthia told me. "Before we got married, Prentice got laid off, and he was crying. He had never asked to borrow money, but he had seemed so hurt that I wrote him a check for something ridiculously reasonable like five hundred dollars. When I got home, there was a message on my answering machine that said, 'You don't know how hard it is for me to ask you for help. You don't know how much I appreciate you, you're so special, so generous.'"

After a few months of marriage and Prentice's rising expectations, Cynthia says of the man who was grateful for five hundred dollars, "I want to know where that person went." According to Cynthia, "There is a huge difference between growing up with money and coming into it through marriage. Prentice's family had a little bit of money, but not what I call 'fuck you money.' 'Fuck you money' is the kind of wealth that allows to you be totally independent and never need to please anyone else to support yourself or your family. One of the things Prentice loved about me was that I was so normal about my wealth. I never felt entitled or acted snobby about it, which I know some rich people do. In fact, when we bought a house, we didn't want one that was ostentatious. I told the broker that I wanted a house that one of my least wealthy friends would be comfortable in. Now Prentice is starting to complain about the size of the house, to ask me to buy him a Mercedes. He used to live with two roommates, and all of a sudden it's a piece of shit house. My shrink says he's saying, 'I don't want you to have all the power, show me that you're going to give me the power.'"

Few women have the kind of money that Cynthia has, but women who make more than their husbands must understand that they are treading on tender egos. Saying things like, "you don't pull your weight," even in anger, is as hurtful as the imperious husband who wants to make all the rules. Couples like Cynthia and Prentice need to find a way to equalize the imbalance of power if they want their marriages to survive.

In my household, I am the one who pays the bills, not because I want to, but because my wife tells me she isn't good at it. By saying this, she has set up what I believe is a negative dynamic in our relationship. Fortunately, we have enough good in our marriage to overcome this problem, but it's not healthy for only one person to be involved in the family's finances. Paying bills takes time from my work, but more important, it makes it difficult for me to explain to my wife why we don't have money for certain things. If she paid the bills, she'd have a better understanding of our cash flow.

Money ignorance can come back to haunt the widow who suddenly has to pick up the bookkeeping duties after fifty years of letting her husband do it. Whatever the reason, it is never good to be in the dark about your personal finances. Even if you're not paying the bills, know what's going on. Every marriage should strive to be an equal partnership regardless of how much you make.

In addition to a power struggle, money can mask what's really going on in a relationship. Couples find it easier to argue about money than about what's really bothering them. I've had men tell me that they become upset when their wives won't have sex with them, so they yell at them for buying new shoes. Likewise, women have complained that they are dissatisfied with their sex lives so they shop to make themselves feel better.

Do not overlook the real problem. Money is one way that couples deceive each other. A woman in my synagogue complained to me that her husband lost their savings gambling, and another said her husband was borrowing money behind her back. Is this about money? No. It's about a couple's inability to be open and honest with one another. It's about using money as a weapon to get back at your partner.

If money is a major source of conflict in your relationship, you need to ask what the fight is *really* about. Is it about power? Is it about not getting what you want? Is it about not valuing yourself? Is it about your feelings of deprivation or being spoiled as a child? Is it about your dissatisfaction with your work or home life?

Once you isolate the problem, you must then ask how it can be solved by working together. Everyone knows a marriage will fail if you don't do the work necessary for keeping it healthy. Like your body, if you don't feed it right or exercise it often, it will go flabby or fail on you. I implore you not to let these problems fester and grow worse with time. Get help. As with any serious marital dispute, professional counseling can be invaluable.

LOVE DON'T COST A THING

Most of the single women in my congregation are professionals, but most tell me they want to stop working eventually to raise children, and they need to find someone who is able to provide for them. I've only met a few women who believe that they can work, rear children, and earn enough to take care of themselves, regardless of the men in their lives.

Part of a woman's desire to marry a good provider is

actually a biological imperative. According to David Buss, Ph.D., professor of psychology at the University of Texas at Austin, women place a high premium on a mate's ambition, industriousness, and social status to help ensure the survival of the species.

Gold digging is another story. As one of my rabbinical school professors told his students on graduation day, "If you marry for money, you'll pay for everything you get." Good advice. What does it mean to marry for money? It means you don't trust your own capacity to provide for yourself. It means you are willing to sacrifice real spiritual and often emotional satisfaction for comfort.

It's like the joke about the woman from Miami who was searching for a wealthy husband. She sat on a bench at the water's edge with a pale, well-dressed man in his forties, who was wearing an expensive gold Rolex. "Why are you so white?" the woman asked.

"I've been in jail for ten years," he replied.

"Ten years! For what?" she asked

"For killing my third wife," he explained. "I strangled her."

"What happened to your second wife?"

"I shot her."

"And, if I may ask, your first wife?"

"We had a fight, and I pushed her off a building."

After taking a few minutes to absorb the information, the woman leaned closer to the man and whispered, "So does this mean you're now a single man?"

Admittedly, life is easier when you are wealthy. Money helps with job losses, illnesses, weddings, tuition, and the mortgage. For most of us, during some years we will have more money than we will during others. But the kind of person we want to be, and the kind of person we want to be with, should be happy with money and happy without it.

Women who marry for money instead of love must learn to live with a certain degree of unhappiness. Men do the same thing with physical beauty. They are willing to accept loveless marriages in exchange for trophy wives. How much do you value yourself if you love money more than you love your husband? How much do you value yourself if you marry someone who loves your money more than she loves you? Do you feel undeserving of true love?

If you are a woman who is marrying for money, understand that you are cutting off a large group of potentially great men (even Bill Gates didn't start out rich) and that you have chosen comfort over love. If you are a man dating someone who you fear might be interested only in your money, stop buying her expensive gifts and dinners. If she stops taking your phone calls, you know where she stands. Remember, the more conspicuous you are with your wealth, the more you are dangling the bait that will attract the wrong person with the wrong values.

It's important to know what you want from a relationship, and I don't fault people for whom money or looks is part of the equation. But I do fault those who doubt their ability to care for themselves and those who believe that their earning power is their greatest asset. What are you going to want from your partner ten, twenty, or thirty years from now? Isn't the idea of marriage about the value of love over all else?

I understand that love doesn't always last forever in a marriage, and that there are such things as irreconcilable differences that you were unaware of when you entered into the union. But when couples ask me about prenuptial agreements, I tell them that they shouldn't get married.

Are there exceptions? Of course. The elderly person who wants to make sure his or her money goes to his or her children might need one, or someone who wants to compensate the spouse who will raise the children for lost wages. But, in general, my experience with couples involved in prenups is almost always ugly.

When a couple comes to me about a prenup, I ask them if they have truly grown to know and trust one another. A prenuptial agreement shows a lack of faith in the potential of the relationship and a lack of faith in each other's motivation for marriage. The bottom line is if you are thinking about getting a lawyer involved in your marriage, take some time before you walk down the aisle. Cynthia, the heiress, didn't want a prenup when she married Prentice because she said she hates talking about money. Her brother got one when he got engaged, and it nearly broke off the marriage.

Whenever I meet a couple that has been married for more than fifty years, I always ask them how they have managed to stay together for so long. One man jokingly said, "Well, we have an agreement that whoever wants to get divorced has to take the kids." A woman who has been in a sixty-year marriage told me, "You have to care about the other person more than you care about yourself." Another long-married, crusty old man told me,

"There are only three words you need to stay married as long as I have: yes, my empress!"

If ever a couple understood what it takes to stay married, Bob and Judy were it. I met them at the end of a floatplane trip deep in the Alaskan wilderness. Most of the year, they live on a forty-foot boat surrounded by nothing but forest and water. There are no roads, and it's one hundred miles by plane to the nearest neighbors.

Occasionally, fishermen from one of the lodges one hundred miles away will fly in to the bay where Bob and Judy anchor their boat to spend the day halibut fishing with them. Bob and Judy never really know on any given day during the fishing seasons whether or not they will have company. Often, the weather is too lousy for flying. Most of the time, Bob and Judy are alone, day after day, with nowhere to go but a forty-foot boat.

Bob is tall and wiry. His skin is leathery and sunburned beneath his eyes, and his hands are scarred and as rough as sandpaper. He smells like halibut and diesel. Judy is pretty in a plain sort of way. Thin, her dirty blond hair is streaked with gray. She has sparkling blue eyes and a kind smile that is lined with the weather and age. She smells like halibut and diesel too.

After an hour or so of uneventful fishing, I can't help but ask them the obvious question. "How do you guys make this work? Just the two of you out here alone for months on only forty feet of boat. How do you stay married?"

"Well, you have to be pretty good friends to begin with," Judy tells me. "Then, there's just one simple thing you have to be able to do to stay on this boat and stay in love. Get over it. Whatever it is that's bothering you, whatever it is the other person said or didn't say, did or didn't do—get over it."

I think about Judy's answer as I continue to fish. Halibut fishing is boring most of the time. It involves dropping a huge, squid-baited hook approximately one hundred fifty feet down, just shy of the bottom. Then, you stand for hours lifting the hook a few feet and letting it settle back down near the bottom again. Lift and settle, lift and settle, lift and settle, while the waves in the bay rock to the sea's gentle rhythm. Like I said, it's boring.

Until you hook a halibut. Halibut can run up to one hundred fifty or two hundred pounds. You know you're in for some fun when you look at the bend in your rod and someone shouts those three marvelous words: "Get the belt!" The belt is a leather and Velcro contraption with a little pouch in front to hold the end of the rod. The belt gives you leverage and takes the load off your forearms and back. The belt means you're in for an hour of pulling and sweating, give and take, until someone shouts out three more wonderful words: "It's a shooter!"

A "shooter" refers to a fish so large you actually have to shoot it with a shotgun when it gets alongside the boat. If you don't shoot it before you hoist in on board, it can send you crashing to the deck with a smack of its tail. Shooters are rare. Most of the time, it's lift and settle, lift and settle, with an occasional twenty-five-pounder easily pulled up on deck in a matter of minutes.

I never feel cheated if the fish are few or small. For me, shooters aren't what it's all about. I like the monotony of it all. The calm. The way the light dances off the blue-gray water. The modest pursuit of quiet, connection, and sway. Lift and settle, lift and settle.

Strange as it sounds, I think marriage is a lot like halibut fishing. Like a shooter, there's the occasional excitement—a wedding, a baby, a first home—but mostly it's a lot of lifting and settling, working together with the rhythm of life rather than against it. It's the way my wife looks in her flannel pajamas at seven in the morning making school lunches for the kids. It's the way we can sit at dinner without having to talk and how much I want to call her every time I'm alone in the car. It's the way I look at her after seventeen years and say with a deep sense of satisfaction, "We're old and married." It's about how good we have become at forgiving each other.

Virtually every couple I ask says the same thing in slightly different ways. It always comes down to putting the other person's needs before your own, learning to let go and get over it. Ask yourself which do you want more at the end of the day and at the end of your life—a bank account bursting at the seams, or a marriage overflowing with love?

Sometimes we can all lose sight of what matters. I did years ago, when my wife and I were taking a short vacation. We had two entire days off from my responsibilities as a rabbi at our temple camps in Malibu and Betsy's job as the assistant arts and crafts director. It had been three long, hot, exhausting, tough weeks working with one hundred twenty hormones-gone-berserk junior high school kids. At the same time, we were caring for our then fourteen-month-old son and eating camp food, which consisted mainly of macaroni and cheese, lumpy oatmeal, and processed chicken patties. We were living in a tiny, rickety trailer.

We needed a break, and we were finally getting one. Two whole days to ourselves in Palm Springs. We even left the baby behind with a sitter. Just the two of us, the desert, the mountains, our favorite Chinese restaurant, going to the movies, and relaxing by the pool.

But halfway to Palm Springs, the warning light on our car told us the engine was overheating. A short in the electrical system we had fixed just a few days prior was back again. The engine fan suddenly shut down and the radiator boiled over. We stopped. I turned off the air conditioning despite the 104-degree heat, filled the radiator with water, and we continued on our way.

Once in Palm Springs, sweat-drenched and fuming, we took the car to a garage to be fixed. That's when we heard the bad news: the compressor was out and would take a few days and hundreds of dollars to fix. Hotter and angrier, we returned to my parent's condominium, where we were staying.

At the end of our patience, our checking account, and our vacation, we headed for the pool beneath a blazing afternoon sun, hoping for a few minutes of peace. We sat on a step, allowing the lukewarm water to lap over us. The unforgiving desert air was still and oppressive.

The quiet of the desert got us thinking. Now that he wasn't with us, we realized just how much work our infant son was. How drained we were from constantly providing for his every need. We wondered why we were living in an expensive city like Los Angeles. How did anyone our age afford a house there? And, for that matter, how would we find the money to fix the car? Maybe my fourteen-hour work days, the worry, and the hurry and the scurry of everyday life was the way it would be forever. Life was too hard, too frustrating. What did we really have to show for it anyway?

Just then a voice beckoned from the pool, "What do you hear from your dad?" We turned to see my parents' neighbor, Rubin, with liver spots on his balding head and a grainy face showing every one of his seventy-four years in the desert sun. "Life is pretty damn hard," he groaned, settling on the step below us.

"We know," I said. "Betsy and I were just talking about it. There never seems to be enough time or money—just a lot of struggle."

When Rubin heard this, his face dropped with a combination of anger, sadness, and wisdom. "Life isn't hard for you," he said dismissively. "Let me give you an old man's advice. As long as you've got someone who really loves and cares for you, as long as you're not alone, life isn't hard. Don't worry about money or houses or anything else. None of it matters.

"My wife's gone and I just can't get over it. She suffered with cancer for three months. She was so beautiful—such a friend. She didn't marry me for the money. I never had much. I'm just a retired warehouse manager. We put everything we had into this condo. Got all Chinese-like furniture for it in L.A. She shot herself in the bathtub because she knew she was going to die soon, and she didn't want to put me through it. Can you imagine that? She didn't want me to suffer watching her die.

"She loved the world and the world loved her. She was

my best friend. Let me tell you kids something. You don't have problems. You've got each other, and you've got people who love you. The money, the job, none of it matters. It all comes and goes."

Betsy and I left the pool humbled by what Rubin had told us. Suddenly, the car, the bills, the heat, and the everyday struggle of life didn't matter anymore. We were simply thankful that we had each other. "God, I love her," I thought to myself. "What's any of it worth without her?"

Rubin was right. He came to us like an angel, a mystic in the desert sun, and he told us exactly what we needed to hear. Life isn't about a career, the house, the cars, the bills, and the struggle. It's about knowing there's at least one person in the world who loves us and that person is ours to love back. It's about the ability to forgive and to let go. It's about the lifting and the settling, holding hands come what may.

CHAPTER FOUR

Teach Your Children
Well, Not Wealth

"THE SUREST WAY TO MAKE LIFE DIFFI-
CULT FOR A CHILD IS TO MAKE LIFE
TOO EASY."

‖ A FATHER AND SON WERE WALK-
ing down the street when they come across the town
drunk and his son lying in the gutter. "Look," said the
boy to his father, "both the father *and* son are drunkards.
What shame!"

"I only hope," said the father, "that I manage to be as
great an influence on you as that man has been on his
son."

It's a silly joke, but with a serious message. Parents are
their children's greatest role models. And when it comes
to money, like blue or brown eyes, our recessive and
dominant fears, ambitions and expectations are directly
inherited.

Our children learn about money by example; what we
say about it, how we save it, give it away, and how much
time and energy we spend acquiring it, all of which can
and should consciously be controlled. It is up to us, as
parents, to teach our children that a full, meaningful life
comes from work, education, and concern for others—
not from material excess.

My father, Leonard, was a blue-collar sort of guy,
who, throughout my childhood, went to work in steel-
toed boots and a uniform that said "Len" on it. His views

on money were based on the time and circumstances of his own childhood. My dad grew up on welfare during the Depression, and he barely finished high school. His family used to burn wax paper in the winter to stay warm. He is a very smart guy when it comes to money.

When I was five years old and wanted a toy, my dad had me shine his dress shoes for a dime a pair. At ten years old, I went to work with him every Saturday morning, cleaning the toilets and floors at the scrap yard he owned with my uncle Mort: no mop or machines, just a pail and a scrub brush. My knees and hands hurt at the end of the day.

Each summer, I wire-brushed the rust off the dumpsters used to hold metal at the scrap yard. Afterward, I painted them black: no paint guns or sprayers, just a roller and a pan. One of those summers, my brother and I spent the evenings crawling in the attic of our Minnesota home pouring bags of insulation into rafters. It was over one hundred degrees up there, and we sneezed out black dust at the end of each shift. Sometimes I slopped tar on the roofs of my father's warehouses in the hot August sun.

Once I helped roof our house. Sometimes I mixed cement by hand in a wheelbarrow to patch the sidewalk. Sure, we could have rented a cement mixer, but my father preferred that I use the "arm-strong" method, as he liked to put it.

My dad was the kind of guy who'd come outside when I was playing with my friends in the street and make me go back into the yard to weed around the shrubs because I hadn't done it right the first time. He was also the kind of guy who'd do the same thing again because I hadn't done it right the second time. Believe me, the third time, you couldn't find a weed around those shrubs with a microscope and tweezers.

My father's solution to every problem great or small was always annoyingly simple and unshakable: work harder. By today's standards, his work ethic might seem excessive, but, for him, work was redemptive and holy.

In a way, it's similar to the ancient rabbis' use of the book of Leviticus in the Bible. The first lessons in a Jewish school were not the magical, wonderful, exciting stories of creation, Adam and Eve, Noah, plagues, and parting seas, but, rather, this grisly, boring book about the sacrifices offered up by our ancestors to God on the altar of the ancient Temple in Jerusalem. Leviticus is a reminder to do the dirty work, to make real sacrifices, then, and only then, to reap the rewards.

It wasn't easy being my father's son, pulling weeds while other kids played in the street. But now I realize that anything I have or will become is a result of the lessons he taught me about hard work. And I realize, too, that we only really care about the things for which we are willing to sacrifice.

One of the great human truths is that we value less what is easy to come by. If something is given away, we look on it with suspicion. There is nothing like seeing your child buy a fifty dollar X-Box game with his or her own bills and coins that he or she earned and saved, and sharing this sense of accomplishment. I think about this when it comes to teaching my own children about money. Although my methods might be quite different from my father's, the basic message remains.

Reinforcing positive messages about the value of hard work is important, but it's equally important to undo negative lessons when we see our children or others making poor decisions. My son recently told me about a young boy who bought a video game for fifteen dollars, played it for a week, and then sold it to another young boy at his school for forty dollars. Clearly, the boy buying the game had no idea of its real value, and the boy selling the game had no problem taking advantage of the situation. Apparently, when the parents of the boy who sold the game for an unfair price heard about it, they just laughed.

I could have gone two ways with my son on this one. Either I could have told him that buying low and selling high, buyer-beware, profit, profit, profit is the right way to live, or I could have told him that a seller is entitled to a reasonable profit, but not entitled to take advantage of another person's ignorance or naïveté. I chose the latter. I told my son that what the boy did who sold the game was wrong. It's wrong to take unfair advantage of another person. Our children have no one but us to teach them that immorality is too high a price for anything.

PRESENCE VERSUS PRESENTS

The Bible teaches that on the seventh day God rested. This is why many Christians do not go to work on Sunday, and many Jews do not work on Saturday. "My father always said that the Sabbath was a day of reflection," says Lynne Price Frenkel of Stamford, Connecticut. "But it's much more than that. On Saturdays, my children look forward to their walks with their father as much as I did with mine when I was a child."

Are we spending all our time at work? Are we reading about the stock market on our days off, or are we reading to our children? Are we as entrepreneurial about our time as we are about our money? For all of us parents out there who are too busy saving the world, the company, or the project on which we're working, I offer the following advice: go home. Many a rabbi and minister has observed that precious few people die wishing they had spent more time at the office. The office will be the office forever; your children won't be children forever.

Pay attention. Really *look* at your children. Listen to what they are telling you and what they are not telling you. What are they saying with their body, their tears, and their laughter? How quickly do they come to the door when you get home? Are you home when you are at home? Or are you hiding behind your work, newspaper, or 120 television channels?

Give your children the gift of your time. Do stuff together, especially the boring stuff like grocery shopping, feeding the dog, taking out the trash, or washing the car. Just "hanging out" with your kids is just as important as doing something "special."

Kids need presence, not presents. Guilt-ridden parents often overcompensate for their absence with elaborate gifts. Unfortunately, a wrapped gift will never take the place of your rapt attention. When it comes to gifts, it's okay to limit the amount and the cost. If you are throwing a birthday party, for example, put a ten- or twenty-dollar gift limit on the presents. I know that twenty dollars doesn't go as far as it used to go, but you'd be surprised how much fun kids can have with simple, inexpensive toys.

In truth, part of the fun is opening the gifts. The surprise, the colorful paper, the oohs and the ahhhs all contribute to the gift-giving (and receiving) experience. How many times have you bought that expensive toy that all the kids on the block want, only to find it in the back of your kid's closet a week later? Almost every parent, sooner or later, has the experience of watching his or her child play with a large, cardboard box from a refrigerator or other appliance. The box becomes a space ship, a car, a fort, a slide, a plane—it's a study in imagination and curiosity. It's children at their best. We, as parents, are at our best when rather than filling our children's rooms with stuff, we leave room in our children's lives for simple pleasures and play.

How Not to Raise a Demon Seed

Parents who are obsessed with money will raise children who are equally obsessed. According to the owners of Imagine Party and Events in Scarsdale, a wealthy suburb of New York City, bar and bat mitzvah parties can cost between fifty thousand dollars and one million dollars if the parents decide, let's say, to transform a warehouse into a Caribbean island or send the guests to an actual Caribbean island.

When I meet with families whose children are about to become a bar or bat mitzvah, I do an experiment. I draw a line down the middle of the blackboard and say, "On the left side of the board, list all the values that are expressed on the pulpit." Almost always, the parents and kids come up with the right answers: learning, tradition, family, spirituality, prayer. Then, I say, "On the right side, list all the values being expressed at the party celebration afterward." They're hesitant, but I don't let up until they make the list: conspicuous consumption, noise, gluttony, excess.

Of course, the problem of excess at rite-of-passage parties is not unique to the Jewish community. In South America, parents often tap into their savings for the *quinceaneros,* a celebration that marks the day their daughters turn fifteen. American parents buy two-thousand-dollar gowns and rent stretch limos for their teenagers' high school proms. According to an article in the *New York Times,* one young man from Minneola, New York, rented a Truckousine—a stretch Ford 350 pickup truck with a Jacuzzi and a bed. He conceded that his father, "thought it was a little ridiculous," but his dad gave his son his approval as well as his credit card.

Some parents even spend thousands on children's birthday parties. A listing on *www.Urbanbaby.com,* a Web site for New York City parents, captured this out-of-control excess in this unabashed posting: "We all know that one-upmanship is especially cutthroat in the world of kiddie birthday bashes," the blurb read. "Why not forget the party bags filled with plastic water guns and cheap crayons (so last millennium), and send your invitees home with something as unique and memorable as a caricature? Rebecca Miller of the Rhode Island School of Design, will come to your kid's party and quickly draw every guest, no matter how squirmy and covered in ice cream. Art, entertainment, and party favor in one, the caricatures can be put on mugs, T-shirts, mouse pads, and magnets. Or simply framed as a mini-masterpiece for your little narcissist." Do we really want to raise mini-narcissists? When did narcissism become chic?

What kind of lesson do these extravagances relay to our children? It teaches them that it is better to be ostentatious than thoughtful. It teaches them to care about appearances and affectation instead of the core values of tradition, spirituality, and family. Sadly, many, many parents fail to realize that the surest way to make adulthood difficult for their children is to turn them into what one psychologist calls "hot house flowers." When we overprotect and overindulge our kids, we weaken, rather than strengthen, them.

I've been married for seventeen years. I swear I don't remember what we had for the wedding dinner. I don't remember what color anything was, or whether we had tulips, orchids, or roses. I don't remember what the invitation said, who sat where, or what the cake looked like. I do remember worrying about those things and my in-laws spending emotional and financial energy on them.

I have officiated at hundreds of weddings. Ironically, 90 percent of what people spend their time and money on is literally garbage the next day. The food, the flowers, the invitations—they all get thrown in the trash. Sadly, people don't spend enough time focusing on what does last—the memories of the ceremony, the faces of loved ones in the room, simple vows, and the affirmation of love.

Don't get me wrong. I like a nice party, good food, and music as much as the next guy does. The problem arises when the true, inner meaning and values of an event are overshadowed or obliterated by excess. The fact is that if you eat too much pie, no matter how delicious, you are going to get sick. This sickness now has a name, thanks to Jesse H. O'Neill, who first diagnosed the problem of "affluenza" in her book, *The Golden Ghetto*.

O'Neill, the granddaughter of an automobile tycoon, defines it as "a dysfunctional or harmful relationship with money and wealth or its pursuit." The symptoms, she says, are listlessness, bad temper, low self-esteem, unchecked egotism, and drug addiction. Sadly, when it comes to the affluenza virus, those who are hit the hardest are our children.

When I asked a young woman who had inherited more than twenty-five million dollars from her grandfather—some when she was in high school, some when she was in her thirties—what the worst things about having money were, she said, "Having money sometimes means you don't have to make choices about what to do with your life. Maybe I would have been a great congresswoman, but to do that, I would have had to go to law school. I could have done that, but I didn't because the motivation to 'make a living' wasn't there.

Having a lot of money at a young age also means you're always questioning people's motives. You're never really sure why they are around you. In older people, money and ambition tend to go together. In younger people, it's just the opposite. I grew up with a lot of kids who felt like they earned it because their parents earned it, which is totally not the case. They do nothing but go from party to party. What kind of life is that?"

No matter how much money you may have, spoiled children, or children who will act immorally for money, are made, not born. Often, a child's unhealthy money issues are a surprise to parents. One of my closest friends, a thoroughly decent man, recently discovered that in his absence, his teenage son threw a party at his home. Word spread about the party, and soon it grew into a three-hundred-kid, out-of-control rave with rock bands and alcohol. After the police broke the party up, my friend discovered that his son's motivation for throwing the party was primarily money. This boy goes to school with kids who have much more materially than he and his family have, and he saw the party as a way to charge admission, make money, and afford some of the things the other kids' parents lavish upon them. Here was a great kid willing to lie to his parents and break the law in order to make some money.

When my friend called me in despair about his son's poor judgment, I told him that he had just been handed a great opportunity. He now had the chance to teach his son that how you make money is as important as how much money you make. Some parents might have laughed this incident off as a teenage prank, but I see it as a crucial moment in a young person's life to learn about money and morality.

We have to take these opportunities as parents to help our kids understand the moral paradigms surrounding money. Money is a reflection of your values, and your values will often show up in your children. As in almost everything having to do with kids, the buck, or in this case, the bucks, stop squarely at the parents.

Easier to preach than teach, you say? It's actually quite simple. We start by not being afraid to tell our kids the truth about the money madness we see around us. Then we have to set boundaries when it comes to the "I wants" and other unreasonable requests. If your seventeen-year-old says, "My friend David just got a Mercedes from his parents," you must point out the error that young David's parents have made. You say, "Your friend's parents are spoiling him. And it's wrong. Even if we *could* afford to buy you one of these cars, we wouldn't."

Sure, you run the risk that your judgmental remarks will get back to David's parents, but it's a risk you must take in order to brat-proof your child. It's okay to be judgmental about excess. It's okay to tell your kids that there is such a thing as too much.

If your kids continue to beg you for the new computer game or toy du jour, don't give in just to stop the haranguing. Of course, telling them you can't afford it when they know that you can will raise the needle on their hypocrisy-meter. But refusing to give in with a good response such as, "You can put that on your birthday/holiday wish list," or "Let's think of a way you can earn this," will put an end to many of their "I wants." It shifts the burden from you onto them. Giving your children everything they ask for creates an empty hole in their spirit that they will continually, but unsuccessfully, try to fill. As an addict in recovery who was indulged as a child once told me, "Instant gratification wasn't quick enough for me."

Brats not only grow up to be obnoxious or dysfunctional adults, they tend to be underachievers. How can they be independent when they haven't learned how do things for themselves? My congregants occasionally ask me what they should say when their child wants to know how much money they make. A good answer to this question might be: "We make enough for everything that we need," which is what I tell my kids.

If you are wealthy and your children ask you if you are rich, don't lie to them (they're not stupid; they know they have more money than most of their friends), but don't exaggerate the importance of money. Tell them, "We are wealthier than many people, and not as wealthy as others. There will always be someone who has more money than you do, so keeping score is a waste of time and says something negative about the kind of person you are."

Never tell young children exactly how much you make—little kids can't really conceive of figures. If you're doing your job right, twenty dollars should seem like a lot of money to a youngster.

And if you hear your children bragging to their friends about their big house or car, stop them in midsentence. Tell them, "This is not your house and car. This is *my* house and *my* car. I earned this house by working hard for it." Tell them that they are acting like snobs and that bragging is ugly and it hurts other people's feelings.

Similarly, don't be afraid to point out to your kids when grownups are being crass about money. If we heard someone making a racist remark, we would tell our kids that that person is ignorant and wrong. Haughtiness, arrogance, and snobbery are all bad traits, and it is our obligation to tell our children that it is reprehensible to engage in that kind of talk or behavior.

While preventing a child from becoming spoiled in the first place is the best solution, what do you do if your kid is already a brat? In this case, the question is not how am I going to change my child, but what do we do to change our family. How are we going to change our priorities so that we teach our child about what is truly important in life?

Take a long, hard look at the way you live. It's not just a matter of saying no to your son or daughter, which is important, but you must also say no to yourself. If you think you might be having what I call an Extra Material Affair, try the following exercise. For a period of two weeks, keep a notebook with you at all times. Write down every time you think or talk about money. (This includes whenever you turn on CNBC to watch the stock ticker.)

Ask your spouse or a friend to tell you if your conversation turns in this direction. You may be surprised at how much of your time and energy is spent pursuing and talking about money. Becoming aware of your thoughts about money is the first step toward changing your behavior.

MAKING ALLOWANCES

Allowances that are earned rather than given teach children early on about the value of work and responsibility. Plus, it's a lot easier to spend someone else's cash. If it took some time and effort to earn their money, your kids might want to hold onto to it a bit longer. I'm not saying that we shouldn't give to our children out of love, but bottomless giving without earning breeds entitlement.

Neale S. Godrey, the kids and money guru, devised an excellent allowance plan for parents with young children. Start them immediately on the "jar system." Each week, kids can work around the house to earn an allowance that is then divided into different jars. Those jars can be labeled College, Charity, Fun Stuff (there should always be fun stuff), and Pocket Cash. Except for emergencies, the money in the jars can't be touched until they reach a certain level, after which they can select the charity of their choice.

Teaching your kids the value of work should start early on. At the very least, children (starting at about age eight) should be required to make their bed in the morning and clean up their toys when they are finished playing. As children get older, parents should insist that they do real work around the house. If you have household help, reserve some tasks for your children such as washing the dishes, raking the leaves, or straightening up their rooms.

Parents can rotate chores each week such as walking the dog, dishes, weeding, and the like so that one sibling doesn't always get stuck with one task. If the chores aren't done, no allowance that week. Think of it this way: if you didn't show up for work (and you're not sick or on vacation), would you expect to get paid?

As far as credit cards are concerned, unlimited credit lines are like handing your child a financial grenade. Do not give your child a credit card until he or she goes to college. Start with a debit or secured card that has a limited credit line based on the money that is deposited in a bank or savings account. That way, if your child defaults, your credit isn't damaged and the payment is taken directly from the account. Likewise, car insurance and gas should come out of your child's allowance, not out of your wallet.

Cell phones are necessary for safety reasons, especially if your child drives a car, but bills can run up fast. I suggest giving your children a cellular phone that has a prepaid chip. If they chat beyond their allotted time, then they are out of luck until the next month.

By the time your kids are teenagers, you should do your best to encourage (or demand) that they get a summer job or part-time work after school. It will give them spending money for clothes, cell phone bills, or whatever they want. It keeps them from being bored, and it teaches them about what it's like to be in the workforce.

Unfortunately, the trend among wealthy families is to extend childhood as long as humanly possible. According to the most recent Bureau of Labor Statistics, only 62 percent of fifteen- to nineteen-year-olds were working, compared to 73 percent in 1978. Add to this another study from Ohio State University that estimated that 9.8 million American teenagers receive cash from their parents to the tune of one billion dollars per week!

It's true that the pressures of children's lives have changed, and kids are exposed to far more outside dangers than we had to cope with growing up. School, especially private school, is extremely competitive. As a result, grownups want their kids to enjoy the joys of childhood rather than add to their stress.

But this kind of thinking creates a lethal cocktail of boredom and untapped youthful energy. It also means that teenagers are being robbed of the opportunity to experience menial work, something my father was determined to teach me. Why should anyone, least of all your beloved offspring, do blue-collar work if they don't have to?

Because there is a kind of social leveling that occurs when college-bound kids get a taste of working-class life. It prevents children of privilege from believing they are "too good" to do certain kinds of work.

Besides, if you are going to be a manager some day, it is important to know what it's like to have a boss. And after flipping enough burgers, your teenagers will be motivated to supersize their brains in college so that they never have to do that kind of work again.

If your teenagers complain about having to work during the summer break, tell them this story about a man named Sigmund Wollman told by the minister Robert Fulghum:

> Wollman was the night auditor at a little inn in Northern California. Every summer the inn employed college students to help out. It seems the owner of the inn fed the employees the same thing for two weeks—every lunch and every dinner the same thing. Two wieners, a mound of sauerkraut, and stale rolls. To add insult to injury, the owner made them pay for their meals by deducting the cost from their paychecks.

Finally, one of the students had reached his limit and started to complain to Wollman. "That's it," he yelled. "I can't stand sauerkraut and wieners, and who eats this stuff even once let alone for two weeks? A pig couldn't take this crap. I hate the owner, I hate the guests, I hate this food. I quit!"

All through the young man's rant, Sigmund Wollman, the night auditor, sat quietly on his stool, smoking a cigarette, watching with sorrowful eyes. Put a bloodhound in a suit and tie and you have Sigmund Wollman. He's got a good reason to look sorrowful. He survived Auschwitz. He's thin, coughs a lot, and likes being alone at the night job with no one telling him what to do. He likes the peace and quiet. Even better, he liked the fact that he could go into the kitchen whenever he wanted to and have all the wieners and sauerkraut he could eat. To him, it was a feast. In Auschwitz he would dream of such a time.

"You know what's wrong with you?" Wollman told the young man when he finished his tirade. "It's not the wieners and kraut, it's not the boss, and it's not the guests, or even this job. You think you know everything, but you don't know the difference between an inconvenience and a problem. If you break your neck, if you have nothing to eat, if your house is on fire—then you have a problem. Everything else is an inconvenience. Life is inconvenient. Learn to tell the difference. You will live longer. And you won't annoy people like me so much. Good night."

Because of the excess surrounding so many of our kids, even if we ourselves are not guilty of overdoing it for them, they often lose sight of the difference between a problem and an inconvenience. They see people get angry with waiters because their steak wasn't done just right or their pasta wasn't al dente. They see mounds of food thrown away in our homes, at their schools, and in every restaurant in America. What they don't often see are the poor rummaging through dumpsters behind those restaurants.

I used to dismiss my mother when she told me to eat my food because children were starving in Africa. I shouldn't have. Take your kids to work in a food pantry or soup kitchen. Get them in touch with those who have less. Help them to realize the difference between a problem and an inconvenience. They'll be better people for it.

A MATTER OF TRUST

If your child isn't a good human being by the time he or she is twenty years old, it's probably too late. This doesn't mean you give up on them; parents never give up on their children, but in terms of trust and trust funds, be careful.

Money will not ruin someone who has his or her values in place, but it's better to wait before bestowing a great deal of money on your kids. If your children know that they will inherit millions when they are eighteen or even twenty-one, then you are robbing them of their initiative.

Are there any stipulations on receiving this bounty? Do they need to educate themselves or learn a trade? If all they have to do to get the money is to live to the age of consent, then they are not likely to have incentive to do much else.

Some parents believe that they owe their children a comfortable or even a privileged lifestyle simply for having brought them into the world. Parents owe their children an opportunity to reach and fulfill their potential. Ironically, giving them too much actually thwarts their motivation to succeed.

Children are like trees. Trees grow stronger because they are exposed to the wind, the ice, and the rain. As one psychologist friend of mine puts it, "We shouldn't treat our children like hot-house flowers. Hot-house flowers don't do well in the real world."

We've all heard about children of the wealthy falling into a tailspin of depression, drugs, or substance abuse after receiving their inheritance funds. Of course we want to give to our children and grandchildren after we pass on. But we must give wisely and understand why giving too much too soon can destroy our children's souls.

I have an acquaintance who is an artist and the son of an extremely wealthy father. He's about forty years old now, plodding along in his profession without much interest in becoming a success. The reason? He knows that one day soon he will inherit a fortune. Why knock himself out toiling when all he has to do is stay alive long enough to collect his inheritance?

I have another friend who is literally a billionaire, but he has made it clear to his children that they will inherit nothing. All his money, he has informed them, is going to charity. Instead of being resentful, his kids are all tremendously successful business people in their own rights.

It doesn't have to be all or nothing. A better compromise would be to set up a charitable foundation. Your kids can be put in charge of deciding how the money will be spent. This seems to work far better than "incentive trusts" that earmark money on the basis of performance. A child might get more money if he becomes a teacher instead of professional bon vivant. But these kinds of trusts are difficult to administer, and children inevitably resent their parents for trying to control them with money.

One of the biggest mistakes you can make as a wealthy parent is to use your money as a threat to make your children behave in the way you want them to do. Your kids might do what you want, but they will hate you for the rest of their lives.

Cutting off your children will cause irrevocable damage. The only exception to this is when you are sure that your money will go toward drugs, gambling, or some other social disease. Barring that, using the threat of disinheritance as a way to control your children is misguided. If you need to employ such tactics with your kids, you have lost them already.

From the other side, if you are the child of a controlling parent, don't accept money even if it's offered. It's not worth it. If you are beholden to a parent who will constantly tell you what to do, whom to see, where you should live, whom you should marry, don't take the money.

While we certainly owe our children some of what we've accumulated through life, and material wills are an important way to do this, I believe that we owe our children more. In Judaism, there is a custom of leaving an "ethical will," which is essentially a letter to your children about the values you hope that they inherit from you. Written ethical wills date back to eleventh-century Germany, France, and Spain. We spend so much time accumulating wealth and possessions to leave behind for our children. Why not also leave our children a written account of our hopes and love for them?

Here is part of my own ethical will, which I have only just begun to write for my children. It is a work in progress, and it goes like this:

Dear Aaron and Hannah,
 I want you to know that you and your mother are the joy of my life; all other accomplishments pale in comparison. . . . Live more for today than for tomorrow. Be forgiving to a fault. When you do something, do your very best. Tell many jokes. Always try to have enough money so that you are never afraid of someone having power over you. But use your money to help the needy.

Our children will need our wisdom and our words more than any possession we can leave them. Wisdom is what we owe our children above all else.

Ten Steps to Raising a Decent Human Being

At some point in our children's lives, virtually all parents challenge them to become not merely human, but humane.

What constitutes being a good, decent person? I offer my own humble, ten-step approach to defining and raising a decent human being:

1. *Teach your children what success really means.* The ancient scribes said that when a child is born, he or she is visited by an angel who requires that the child take a simple oath "to be righteous and never be wicked." A child is not asked to be brilliant, cute, athletic, or popular, but, rather, to be kind, honest, and understanding. This means we must think about the things for which we praise our children. Helping a friend, caring for an animal or the Earth ought to be praised as much as good grades or a goal in soccer.

    This is one area that my wife and I have worked very hard on with our daughter Hannah. Hannah has fiery red hair that attracts a lot of attention. Whenever someone stops her in public and says to her, "Your hair is so beautiful," or "You are so cute," we always make a point of asking Hannah directly in front of the person who paid her the compliment, "Hannah, what's more important than being cute? Hannah knows, because we've told her, to answer by saying, "being good," or "being healthy," or "being nice." It's our way of teaching her that we don't care about how cute she is; we only care about how good she is.

2. *Be a decent role model.* Do we tell our children to be honest, but sneak them into the movies for the under-twelve price when they're twelve and a half? Do we tell them we're going out to a meeting, and they later

find out we went to dinner and a movie? Do we tell them to be lawful, and then park in the handicapped spot? Do we tell them to be kind to their brothers and sisters when we haven't spoken to our own siblings in months? Do our children hear us say we care about the poor, and then watch us ignore their outstretched hands and their hungry eyes as we walk by them? Our children might not always be listening to us, but they are always watching.

3. *Treat people as you wish your children to treat them.* Most people are decent to someone from whom they want something, be it friendship, sex, or money. But if our children see us treating everyone decently— from the janitor in the office to the tourist asking for directions—they will do the same. When a man who served as the White House stenographer for more than forty years retired, he was asked for which president he enjoyed working the most. He answered that Harry Truman was his favorite because he was the only president who called him by his name. If you want to raise a decent person, don't treat anyone like they are hired help, even if they are hired help.

4. *A decent person doesn't disappear.* When your child's friend or classmate is sick or experiences a divorce or tragedy, encourage your child to visit, call, or send an e-mail or card. Teach them to reach out to people in need, to those who are sad or troubled, even if they don't ask for help. Teach them to open their human spirit and not to run away or become consumed by their own lives.

5. *A decent person knows the difference between a problem and an inconvenience.* Do our children see us angrier about rush-hour traffic than racism, pollution, or violence? What angers us teaches children about our real priorities. As Robert Fulghum wrote: "Sure, life is lumpy. But a lump in the oatmeal and a lump in the breast are not the same lump." Problem or inconvenience? Teach children the difference so that they don't grow up to be selfish or petty.

6. *A decent person gives more money to charity than he can afford, and more time to the community than he has to spare, but somehow his family always comes first.* Do we have family rituals for our children to rely on and be comforted by? Do we take family time seriously? Do we take the Sabbath seriously with all of its good food, music, blessings, and warmth? It's pretty much everything a child needs.

   A recent study of SAT scores revealed that the single most important factor for high-scoring kids—more important than gender, socioeconomic background, ethnicity, or living in the city or suburbia—was having dinner together as a family at least four nights per week.

   Many privileged families have housekeepers, nannies, gardeners, pool men, car detailers, and therapists taking care of their needs. Children who see this grow up believing that people other than their parents and siblings are essential to everyday life. While none of us wants to deprive our children of the comfort or advantages that money can offer, I do think it's essential that our families have regular sacred time together.

7. *A decent person doesn't prejudge.* What words do your children hear at home? Fag, dyke, bitch, retard, old fart, loser, not to mention a slew of racial and ethnic epithets. If a person is black, white, brown, or some combination of the three, man or woman, young or old, married or single, thin or overweight, straight or gay, a decent person doesn't care. If you do care, so will your children.

8. *A decent person is honest.* Ask yourself this question: if your child, who is an excellent student on her own, gained entrance into an Ivy League school by cheating on one small exam, would you turn her in to the school authorities for doing it? Your answer reveals your child's moral future.

9. *A decent person doesn't gossip.* We gossip about people who are our superiors because it makes us feel somehow better about ourselves to seem in the know, or to have the goods on someone we admire. Unfortunately, gossiping can be hurtful, and it degrades the person who is doing it. The less time children spend gossiping about what others do or do not have the better. That goes for adults too.

10. *A decent person is kind.* A therapist once told me that 90 percent of what she treats people for could have been prevented or cured by ordinary kindness. A kind word, a call, a touch, a hug. The world is starving for kindness. Teach your children to be kind.

CHAPTER FIVE | # Your Money or Your Life?

"THE DAYS ARE LONG. THE YEARS ARE SHORT."

—UNKNOWN

‖ AMERICANS WORK HARD. THE average workweek is sixty hours, and less than a third of all Americans take vacations longer than nine days. Workaholism has gotten even worse since laptops, faxes, e-mail, and cell phones have blurred the line between home and office. People take their cell phones to the beach, to the gym, even to the toilet! We work on airplanes and on commuter trains. What does it do to us physically, psychologically, and spiritually to work all the time? When I say your money or your life, I mean that we decide when our work stops and our life begins. Are we working for a living or living to work?

Sadly, workaholism is the last acceptable addiction, especially for men. We've all seen them, and maybe you are one: online, on target, on budget, on hold, beeper on the belt, up before the kids are awake, home after they are asleep, no decision made without him, no solution possible without him, no problem shared, no burden ever lifted, no friends, no warmth, no love. Try asking a room full of men if they are workaholics, and watch the hands waving in the air. Ironically, we seem to be proud of this behavior.

For many men, work is the best friend, the other

woman, the family, and the child to be raised and nurtured. And for these men, the words from this century-old Yiddish song called *"Mine Yingele"* still holds true today.

> I have a little son, a boy completely fine.
> When I see him it seems to me that all the
>   world is mine.
> But seldom do I see my child awake and bright.
> I only see him when he sleeps, I'm only home at
>   night.
> It's early when I leave for work, when I return
>   it's late.
> Unknown to me is my own flesh, unknown is
>   my child's face.
> When I come home so wearily, in the darkness
>   after day.
> My pale wife exclaims to me, you should have
>   seen our boy at play.
> I stand beside his little bed, I look and try to
>   hear.
> In his dreams he moves his lips, why isn't
>   Daddy here?

This one-hundred-year-old song makes it pretty clear that with all the progress we've made in a century, we haven't come very far when it comes to our inner lives.

Consider this now well-worn story that made the rounds on the Internet some time ago about an American businessman who visits a coastal village in Mexico. He is sitting at the pier when a fisherman in a small boat docks. Inside the boat are two yellow fin tuna. The American compliments the fisherman on the quality of his fish and asks how long it took to catch them.

"Only a little while," the fisherman replies. The American asks why he didn't stay out longer and catch more fish. The Mexican says he had all he needed for his family. The American then asks, "But what do you do with the rest of your time?"

The fisherman says, "I sleep late, fish a little, play with my children, take siesta with my wife, and stroll into the village each evening where I sip wine and play guitar with my amigos. I have a full and busy life, señor."

The American says, "I am a Harvard M.B.A., and I can help you. You should spend more time fishing and buy a bigger boat with the proceeds. With the profits from the bigger boat, you could buy several boats. Eventually you will have a fleet of fishing boats. Instead of selling your catch to a middleman, you could sell directly to the processor and open your own cannery. Once you control the product, processing, and distribution, you would need to leave this coastal fishing village and move to Mexico City, then to Los Angeles or New York, where you will run your enterprise.

The fisherman listened politely. "But, señor, how long will all this take?"

The businessman replied, "Fifteen to twenty years."

"But what then, señor?"

"That's the best part," the American says. "When the time is right, you announce an IPO and sell your company stock to the public and make millions."

"Millions, señor? Then what?"

"You retire to a small coastal fishing village where you sleep late, fish a little, play with your kids, take siesta with your wife, and stroll to the village in the evenings where you could sip wine and play your guitar with your amigos."

BEAT THE CLOCK

Too many of us were taught by our fathers, coaches, or bosses that we can never work too hard or too long. Ultimately, workaholism comes from a lack of self-esteem. If you only value yourself in terms of your job, you are living a narrow, one-dimensional kind of existence. Are you simply a generator of cash, like a human ATM? A person who is willing to live like this doesn't think he or she deserves a full life. You *deserve* a good marriage. You *deserve* good friends. You *deserve* a good family unit. It's part of what God intended for us as human beings.

If there is one tradition that will save our marriages, our families, and our sanity, it is the Sabbath. Every religion has some form of respite, be it attending church services on Sunday if you're Christian, praying five times per day if you are Muslim, or meditating if you are a Buddhist.

Despite what nearly all religions tell us, we often forget that we need to nourish our souls. This is why we must devote at least one day per week to something other than our work. The ancient rabbis thought of it as living a seventh of your life in heaven. By observing the Sabbath, you are essentially calling a truce in the economic battle for existence that most of us wage during the week. It's a way of reclaiming your life as it was meant to be lived.

Think of it this way: keeping the Sabbath fifty-two

Saturdays or fifty-two Sundays per year is the equivalent of seven and a half weeks of vacation! Sounds pretty good when considered that way, doesn't it? But the Sabbath is not about resting so you can do a better job at the office. That would make it just another weapon in the economic battle for advancement. The Sabbath has value in and of itself. For Jews, the Sabbath is the day that we divorce ourselves from our obsession with things. It is a day on which we do no work, use no money, and cease our struggle to acquire more things. It is a day to study, to pray, and to relax with our loved ones. In Judaism, the Sabbath isn't always about what you do, it's about what you *don't* do.

To me, the Sabbath is about having time alone in my prayers to God, a poem, a song, a walk holding my wife's soft hand, or spending time with my children. For others, it could be about pruning roses, listening to a Brahms concerto, having a sumptuous meal, or taking a long nap.

Some people mistakenly believe that to rest is to be lazy, but the Sabbath is not about sloth. It takes a great deal of discipline to observe the Sabbath because it means we must clear a path during the other days of the week for this special day. I guarantee that if we took the Sabbath as seriously as we take our jobs, we would lead far richer lives.

Leading a rich life is dependent upon our ability to understand the value of time. Most of us spend most of our time trying to conquer the material world. We judge our worth by how much of the material world we own. Houses are valued by square footage, not by the warmth and love that dwells within them. But in truth, we all know better. If for example you lost everything you owned in a house fire, the things that would be truly irreplaceable, the things you would miss the most, would be things that actually were of very little monetary value—pictures, mementos, family heirlooms. The things that are really the most valuable are priceless because they represent time, moments shared, and repositories of memories with the people we love. Time is much more valuable than space or money, but most of us live our lives oblivious to this simple, profound truth.

I understand that observing the Sabbath is one of the hardest things to do, but once you start reclaiming this day for yourself, you will never go back.

When people say to me, "But, Rabbi, I *have* to work on the weekends," or "When else can I got shopping?" I tell them that they are not powerless to slow down. We must put limits on the degree to which we are willing to sell our soul for a dollar. The Jewish tradition of "*Cheshbone Hanefesh*" calls for an "accounting of our souls," not our money. We don't need more stuff, more money, or more information; even the least informed among us has more information than a king of two centuries ago did. What we need is more reflection, more silence, and more solitude.

It's like the story of the merchant who had one hundred fifty camels to carry his things and forty servants who did as he ordered. One evening, he invited a friend, Saadi, to join him. The whole night he couldn't get any rest and talked constantly about his problems, troubles, and the pressures of his profession. He talked about his wealth and estates in India and displayed his jewels and the titles to his lands.

"Oh, Saadi," he sighed, "I have another trip coming up. After this trip, I want to settle back and have a hard-won rest. That's what I want more than anything in the world. This trip, I'm going to take Persian sulfur to China because I've heard that it is very valuable there. From there I want to transport Chinese vases to Rome. My ship will then carry Roman goods to India, and from there I will take Indian steel to Halab. From Halab, I will export mirrors and glass to Yemen and take velvet to Persia."

With a sad expression, he then proclaimed to his friend, Saadi, who had been listening in disbelief, "And, after that, my life will belong to peace, reflection, and meditation, the highest goal of my thoughts."

If you are a little like Saadi's friend—and who isn't—try saying this prayer the next time you are about to start your Sabbath:

Lord, ease the pounding of my heart by quieting my mind. Steady my hurried pace. Give me calmness amidst the confusion of my day. Remind me each day of the fable of the hare and the tortoise that I may know that there is more to life than speed. Let me look upward toward the branches of the towering oak and remember that it grew great and strong because it grew slowly. Slow me down, Lord. Slow me down.

In business, there are sacred rules. Never sign a contract without reading it carefully. Always check references. We also need sacred rules in our lives that protect us from losing our souls.

When I was a young rabbi, I worked seven days each week. I was ambitious and I wanted to prove myself by getting people to join my synagogue. An older rabbi, who saw how much I was working, asked me what my typical week was like.

"I'm out four nights a week, I work every day, and at night I write my sermons," I told him.

He looked at me and said, "You know, your congregation has become the other woman in your life. You're cheating on your wife."

He was right. Working too much created difficulties in my marriage and the difficulties in my marriage made me want to work more. It's like that Catch-22, "I drink because I'm unhappy, and I'm unhappy because I drink."

Are you working to feed your family, or are you feeding something negative in your life? We all take pride in a job well done, but it is meaningless if we do it at the expense of our friends, family, and integrity. What is money worth to you? Is it worth not seeing your children? Is it worth a bad marriage? Is it worth immorality?

There are times when we all have to work hard. That's a given. It's also fine to be proud of our careers. But what do you want your headstone to say: "Success at the office, failure everywhere else?" I want mine to say that I was a devoted rabbi, but not nearly as much as I want it to say "devoted friend, husband, father," and hopefully, "grandfather."

Some people see their role on Earth as architects of the material world. Masters of their universe. The folly is that only God can be the master of the universe. As Abraham Joshua Heschel observed, "How proud we often are of our victories in the war with nature. Proud of the multitude of instruments we have succeeded in inventing, of the abundance of commodities we have been able to produce. Yet our victories have come to resemble defeats. In spite of our triumphs, we have fallen victim to the work of our hands; it is as if the forces we have conquered have conquered us. . . ."

I've buried a lot of people—hundreds of them. Each time, I sit down with the surviving family members to talk about their loved one's life. Over the years, I've come to realize that it's rarely the kind of things that you would put on a resume or in an obituary that people tell me about. These conversations with loved ones left behind almost never focus long on professional accomplishments. Instead, we end up talking for hours about the tiniest, intimate, simple moments that people shared with the person who has died. The day he let you skip school and took you to the amusement park. The fishing trips, the ball games, mom driving you to school, Sunday morning breakfast in your pajamas, hot tea on cold winter nights, her smile, the sparkle in his eyes, the sound of her laughing.

No matter how successful, how fulfilling, how powerful our work might be, no matter how great our accomplishments, what do they amount to if our lives are without any time for family and friends? No matter how great our financial bounty, what is it worth without being there for the laughter and tears of our children? We must, as Heschel said, be the architects of time, or moments in time.

Sure, we have e-mail, faxes, voice mail, and palm pilots. We think of these things as progress and, in a sense, they are. But the very things that keep us wired also can fence us off from our inner life. When we lose control of our sacred time we are in danger of losing our souls.

How to Succeed Without Greed

A dog was given a fine meaty bone by a friendly neighbor. On his way home, with the bone firmly between his teeth, the animal had to cross a bridge over a narrow stream. When he reached the middle of the bridge the dog paused to look into the water and saw his own reflection magnified. Thinking that the other dog had a larger bone, the animal decided to take it by force. He leaned over and snapped at his own reflection. As he did so, the bone between his teeth fell into the water and was lost.

—Aesop

The earliest settlers in what was to become America dealt with the difficult task of starting a new country by devising a commonwealth. The idea was to create a society that worked for the communal good rather than for the wealthy few. It was an attempt to separate from the oppressive monarchy under which they formerly lived. Unfortunately, almost immediately after stepping onto dry land, the new citizens of America started to exploit one another. Merchants and laborers gouged the price of lumber after the first cold winter, so the lawmakers put a cap on the amount they could charge to build a house. The greed they thought they left behind in England had followed them to the New World.

When it comes to business, greed, usury, bribery, and embezzlement are as old as civilization itself. And what we are seeing today with the Enrons, Worldcoms, and Tycos is not only greed, but also hubris, which is an exaggerated sense of pride and self-importance. It was hubris that made the heads of these corporations think they had the right to bilk the company coffers for their own personal gain.

People who are dishonest in business are motivated not just by the desire to make millions, but also to feel important. Like the soldier who was promoted to major general and hadn't been in his new office for more than a few minutes when someone knocked on his door. The new major general, wanting to impress the visitor, whoever he was, said, "Come in," quickly picking up the phone on his desk and pretending to have an important high-level discussion.

"Yes, Mr. Secretary, I quite agree," the officer said into the phone, "but perhaps you'd better reserve judgment until I've had a chance to go over the matter. Very good, Mr. Secretary, I'll expect you and your wife at my house this evening for dinner."

After hanging up, the major general turned to the visitor who had been waiting patiently on the other side of his desk. "Yes, young man," the officer said pompously, "What can I do for you?"

"Nothing, sir," replied the stranger. "I was sent here to install your phone."

There will always be those who want to seem important, and there will always be those who want to take more than their fair share. The basic human impulse for greed takes a great deal of character to overcome.

When my brother was studying to become a chef at the Culinary Institute of America, a wholesale butcher who sold his meat to some of New York's finest restaurants guest-lectured the would-be chefs on buying beef. The butcher began his talk by holding up a seven-pound meat hook. "You see this meat hook?" he barked. "These extra seven pounds per sale put my three kids through college."

My brother and I laughed for years about his story because it reminded us of our father and uncle in the scrap metal business. Almost daily some customer would try to cheat them by sitting in his truck while it was weighed. The idea was to get their body weight included in the load, thereby being paid for an extra two hundred pounds or so of metal. This ploy was easily countered, however, by my father. He'd place a current picture of a *Playboy* centerfold right next to the scale dial, thus enabling him to shave off a couple hundred pounds while the driver's eyes were cleverly diverted.

Truth be told, we all want to tip the scale in our favor every now and then. Nevertheless, on the subject of integrity in the marketplace, the Bible warns, "You must have completely honest weights and completely honest measures if you are to endure long on the soil that the Lord your God is giving you. For everyone who does those things, everyone who deals dishonestly, is abhorrent to the Lord your God."

Dealing dishonestly with weights and measures in the marketplace was a serious offense for our ancestors. It meant a breakdown of trust in the community, a never-ending cycle of anger, deception, and revenge in a cheat-or-be-cheated world. It seems a simple, straightforward message. But to believe that the Bible was only telling us to be honest in business would be to miss the subtle brilliance of the sages.

As harmful as dishonest scales in the marketplace might have been, and continue to be, there is another kind of scale and another kind of deception that is far worse. And most of us are guilty of it every day. It's the little things we do that matter most. They mark our success or failure as human beings—the tiny choices we make each day when no one is looking. Isn't that where the game is really won or lost—the everyday temptations?

Were we fair in business when we could have cheated without being caught? Were we kind to strangers we would never see again, in line, in traffic, on the phone? It's the little things that turn us in the wrong direction. "At first evil is as fragile as the thread of a spider," the Talmud says, "but eventually it becomes as tough as cart ropes."

Two thousand years ago, the spiritual leaders of the day determined which parts of our lives were predestined and which depended upon us. According to the ancient rabbis, at the moment of conception, an angel takes the drop of semen from which the child will be formed and brings it before God. "Master of the Universe, what shall be the fate of this drop?" the angel asks. "Will it develop into a strong person or a weak one, a wise person or a fool, a wealthy person or a poor one?"

The angel does not ask if the soon-to-be-formed person will be wicked or righteous. Why doesn't the angel ask God this question? Because the sages believed in something that neuroscientists and psychologists have made unfashionable. They believed something that is no longer politically correct. They believed that we—not our genetic make-up, nor our environment, not even God—are responsible for our moral choices. The genetic fix might be in when it comes to how tall or strong we will be, perhaps even how smart, but not how decent. Our decency is up to us.

There's an old folk tale about a livery driver named Jake. He was passing by a small inn when he realized he was very hungry. That morning he had left his house before sunrise, rushing to make sure his customer would not be late for his train.

After tying his horses to a post and making sure they had hay and water, Jake entered the inn for breakfast. He ate four boiled eggs with a thick slice of bread and butter. He washed it all down with a glass of sweet tea, expertly breaking a piece of sugar between his teeth. But when Jake reached into his pocket for his change purse, he realized he had lost his money through a hole in his pocket. As a result, he could not pay for his breakfast.

"I will stop by when I come this way again," Jake promised the innkeeper. What could the innkeeper do but trust Jake to keep his word?

Months went by and Jake still did not have any occasion to drive by that inn. In time, he forgot his debt. Years passed, and Jake decided to go to the big city, where so many of his relatives had gone before him. They had written to him about the city in such glowing terms, calling it "a golden opportunity," and "a place where the streets are paved with gold." So Jake went to the big city, and, he too, had great fortune. Despite all his wealth, Jake still longed for his home in the countryside. So one day, Jake decided to return to his village.

When Jake arrived at the train station back home, he hired a livery much like the one he once drove to take him to his old house. On the way, he passed the inn where he had eaten several years before and suddenly remembered about his breakfast. "Stop here for a moment," he shouted to the driver. "I must repay a debt I owe."

Jake entered the inn and immediately recognized the innkeeper, although the innkeeper did not recognize him. Jake had become a rich man and dressed like a nobleman. "I have come to pay my debt for breakfast I ate here a few years ago." Jake took out his purse and handed the innkeeper a half-dollar.

The innkeeper took a look at the newly wealthy man wearing such fine clothes and thought greedily about how he could get even more money. "A half dollar!" the innkeeper exclaimed. "What do you mean by paying only fifty cents? Let me give you a complete accounting of what you owe me. Let me see: four eggs would have hatched four chickens, and they each would have hatched sixteen chickens, which makes sixty-four. They, in turn, would have hatched 1,024 chickens, each producing 4,096 chickens . . . "

The innkeeper went on rapidly calculating the amount

until he finally said, "And so you owe me not a half dollar, my friend, but $1,285." The innkeeper insisted on payment, threatening to call the police if Jake did not pay.

"What? How is that possible?" cried Jake. "Do you take me for a fool? How can I pay that amount when I don't have that much money with me?"

The two men agreed to go to a judge's house the next day to decide the case. The innkeeper agreed to let Jake stay at his inn until then. As Jake sat drinking a cup of tea, angered by the injustice of the demands, he was approached by the innkeeper's young and clever daughter. She asked him what was troubling him, and when he told her the story of the debt, she smiled reassuringly at Jake and said, "You are right to feel upset, but don't worry any longer—I have a plan."

The next day, the innkeeper and Jake drove in a carriage to the judge's house. As the judge listened to the innkeeper's case about how much Jake owed him, the door opened and in came his daughter carrying a sack filled with roasted chestnuts.

"Here they are," she said abruptly to the innkeeper, handing him the sack. "I will begin planting tomorrow."

The surprised innkeeper said, "What is this? What are you planting?" He opened the sack and burst into laughter. "Oh, this is a good one! These chestnuts are boiled, you foolish girl. Chestnut trees don't grow from cooked chestnuts!"

"So they don't," answered the daughter, "but neither can boiled eggs be hatched!"

The judge smiled and agreed, "All that Jake owes is half a dollar for the breakfast of four boiled eggs." The innkeeper's reputation for greed spread though the town, and no one ever stopped at the inn again.

The truth is that greed is only temporarily rewarded in the marketplace and in life. Eventually, selfishness catches up to you and destroys your reputation, your family, and your friendships.

Legend has it that there is scale in heaven for each of us: a scale on which our deeds, both good and evil, are measured. And we all have such deeds within us—good and evil, love and cruelty, generosity and selfishness—and we do battle with them all our lives. The heavenly scale may be a legend, but make no mistake: what we do here on Earth is recorded in the memories of our children, who may not always be listening, but who are always watching and who can see into our hearts. This is why the things we do in our personal and work lives are so important. They mark our successes and failures as human beings—these choices that we make each day when no one is looking.

When we're faced with ethical choices about how much to work and how honestly to work, about the time we spend on our inner lives and with our families, we would be well served to consider this chilling reminder from the Talmud. "In the hour when an individual is brought before the heavenly court for judgment," warns that wise book, "the person is asked: 'Did you conduct your business affairs honestly? Did you set aside regular time for study (your inner life)? Did you work at having children (was family important to you)? Did you look forward to the world's redemption (have you left the world better than you found it)?'"

No one understood this better than a member of my

congregation named Sam, whom I visited in the hospital after he had a triple bypass. He was alone in the room when I arrived. The lights were dim, and he looked tired and pale. I stepped in quietly, not sure if he was awake.

"Hello, Rabbi," he said barely louder than a whisper. "It was nice of you to come."

For the next ten minutes or so, I sat by Sam's bed and we exchanged small talk about his surgery, the miracles of modern medicine, his children, and his wife of sixty years. Then, Sam raised himself up a bit and asked, "How are you, Rabbi?"

It seemed an odd question, considering that he was the patient. But Sam is the kind of person who thinks of others first, and because he asked, I decided to answer.

"Well, Sam, to tell you the truth, I've been working all day on my High Holy Day sermon, and I'm frustrated and nervous. Rosh Hashana [the Jewish New Year] is just around the corner, and I don't feel like I have much to say. What would you say on Rosh Hashana if you had the chance, Sam? Tell me what your bypass has taught you."

Two days after his life-threatening surgery, I knew that whatever Sam had to say would be the truth. People in his position have a pretty clear idea of what's important in life. Sam grew pensive, his eyes clear and intense as he laced his fingers behind his head and took a deep, thoughtful breath.

"What this surgery has taught me, Rabbi, is this: if you don't hurt other people, if you lead an honest life, you'll have a good life. Not a perfect life, but a good life. That's what you should tell them in your sermon, Rabbi."

What Sam had to say might seem obvious. But it's a

truth by which it's sometimes hard to live. It's not always easy to do the right thing when no one is watching. The temptation toward selfishness is hard to resist. When I feel it myself, I just remember Sam, who, in his own, simple way, put it best.

MEANINGFUL WORK

A friend of mine, who is also a rabbi, told the following story about a congregant. He was a high-powered lawyer, whose work even involved playing a significant role in the Middle East peace negotiations. Once this former attorney retired, he filled his time volunteering as an ombudsman in a local nursing home. It was his job to handle complaints and to be an advocate for the residents and their families. It was at this nursing home that my colleague bumped into the lawyer.

"I know what you're thinking," the retired attorney told my friend. "I used to be an important person. I functioned at the top levels of business and politics. I was a dealmaker, and now, here I am at this nursing home. But, Rabbi, do you see that man over there? Yesterday, when they served him his lunch, they put a half a cantaloupe in front of him, and thirty minutes, later they came to take it away. I stopped the woman from removing the tray, and I told her, 'This man has had a stroke. He can't eat a cantaloupe like that. You have to scoop it out for him.'

So she did scoop it out into bite-sized pieces. The man slowly lowered his spoon, placed one piece upon it at a time, and gently brought it to his mouth. Rabbi, watching that man eat his cantaloupe was one of the finest moments of my life."

This story is proof, as I've told my children, that meaningful work can be even more rewarding than lucrative work. As poet Maya Angelou said, "Success is liking yourself, liking what you do, and liking how you do it." Even the writer Michael Lewis, who made a fortune while working on Wall Street, came to question his own views on money:

> My father's generation grew up with certain beliefs. One of those beliefs is that the amount of money one earns is a rough guide to one's contribution to the welfare and prosperity of our society. I grew up unusually close to my father. Each evening I would plop into a chair near him, sweaty from a game of baseball in the front yard, and listen to him explain why such and such was true and such and such was not. One thing that was almost always true was that people who made a lot of money were neat—Horatio Alger and all that. It took watching his son being paid two hundred twenty-five grand at the age of twenty-seven, after just two years on the job, to shake his faith in money. He has only recently recovered from the shock.
>
> I haven't. When you sit, as I did, at the center of what has been possibly the most absurd money game ever and benefit out of all proportion to your value to society (as much as I'd like to think I got only what I deserved, I don't), when hundreds

of equally deserving people around you are all raking it in faster than they can count it, what happens to the money belief? Well, that depends. For some, good fortune simply reinforces the belief. They take the funny money seriously, as evidence that they are worthy citizens of the Republic. It becomes their guiding assumption—for it couldn't possibly be clearly thought out—that a talent for making money come out of a telephone is a reflection of merit on a grander scale. It is tempting to believe that people who think this way eventually suffer their comeuppance. They don't. They just get richer. I'm sure most of them die fat and happy.

For me, however, the belief in the meaning of making dollars crumbled, the proposition that the more money you earn, the better the life you are leading was refuted by too much hard evidence to the contrary. And without that belief, I lost the need to make huge sums of money. The funny thing is that I was largely unaware how heavily influenced I was by the money belief until it had vanished.

Golden handcuffs are still handcuffs. I'm not saying that we shouldn't make a lot of money if we're lucky enough to be well compensated for our work. But many of us accept unhappiness in exchange for the sum total of our paycheck. If you think you can't leave, you're wrong. You can always leave. It's fear that keeps us handcuffed to a job. We may have to make less, but what price do we put on happiness?

CHAPTER SIX

He Who Has the Gold Makes the Rules

"TOO MANY PEOPLE SPEND MONEY THEY
HAVEN'T EARNED, TO BUY THINGS THEY
DON'T WANT, TO IMPRESS PEOPLE THEY
DON'T LIKE."

—WILL ROGERS

‖ A LONG TIME AGO IN THE POL-
ish city of Krakow, there lived a man named Avrom.
Avrom had a wife and many children. In their small cottage, there were only two rooms: a kitchen and a bedroom. The bedroom was divided into two parts by a sheet
in the place of a wall. On one side of the improvised wall
was Avrom's bedroom, and, on the other side, was where
the children slept. The kitchen had an earthen floor, which
was covered daily with fresh straw. Everyone loved to
stay in the kitchen because of the black, pot-bellied stove
that warmed them through the long, cold winters.

Avrom was a hardworking man. But no matter how
much he worked, he earned barely enough for the family's
daily needs—food, candles, material for clothing, and lessons for the children. When a dress became too short for
one of the daughters, a pretty, embroidered ribbon would
be added to the skirt to make it longer. And when a pair of
pants became too small for one of the boys, some patches
were sewn on to the worn spots, and the pants would be
passed down to the younger son.

Avrom tried his best. He tried hard not to think of all
the money he owed to shopkeepers and to teachers. So
while he worked, he would often hum to himself or make

up stories about faraway places. Of all his daydreams, Avrom was particularly fond of one. He would sit and think about having the finest meals to which he could invite many guests to share with him and his family.

"Ah," he would say to himself, "come my friends, we have plenty of room and plenty of food for everyone." Avrom would then picture how it would be to have an extra piece of fish. That, he felt, would give him the greatest pleasure.

Just as these thoughts came to Avrom during the day, dreams came to him at night. One night he had an unusual dream. Avrom saw himself standing under a bridge. All around him were magnificent buildings, and one building looked like a palace. Suddenly a voice spoke to him and said: "Avrom, this is the great city of Prague. There is the bridge leading to the king's palace. Dig a hole right where you are standing under the bridge and you will find a treasure."

Avrom suddenly awoke and saw that it was morning. "Prague? How can I go to Prague? I don't even have enough money for my family's needs," he muttered to himself. After a few moments, Avrom realized that it had been only a dream, nothing more. Dreams are nice, he thought, but he had to get to work. His family depended on him.

But all day long, the words of the voice in his dream remained in his mind. The following night, Avrom had the same dream. Again, he heard the voice; only this time it teased him. "Avrom, what are you waiting for? Are you enjoying your poverty?"

The next morning, Avrom told his wife about his

dream. She listened and smiled in an understanding way. "Oh Avrom," she said. "You are such a dreamer! You talk and think of faraway places all day, so why shouldn't you dream about them at night? It's getting late now. You better get to work."

That night, the dream came to Avrom for the third time, but this time the voice in the dream was more insistent. "Avrom! The treasure is there waiting for you. What can you lose by seeing for yourself? Go and take it! It will solve all your problems!"

After the third time, Avrom decided to go to Prague to see if the dream really would come true. Since he had no money to spend on traveling by coach for this foolishness, he would have to go on foot. His wife put some bread and cheese in a sack and filled a bottle with water for the journey.

At dawn, just as the sun was rising, Avrom began to walk the long miles to Prague. During his journey, whenever he was tired, hungry, or discouraged, he would sing praises to God. He knew in his heart that God would protect him. Often he danced little steps along the way, and that made his feet seem less tired.

Finally, weeks later, in the middle of one afternoon, Avrom arrived in Prague. To his amazement, he saw everything just as it had been in his dream. In fact, he had the feeling that he had been there before, but that was impossible. There, in front of him, was the palace of the king, and there was the bridge leading to the palace. It was not a big bridge. Avrom was somewhat disappointed at seeing that it was really so small. But he knew the exact spot where he stood in the dream, so he went and stood there.

Then he noticed that there were palace guards everywhere, and he knew that he had to be careful or they would become suspicious of him.

As Avrom stood there thinking about what to do next, the captain of the guards approached him and demanded to know what his business was. Avrom was bewildered for a moment. Should he tell the guard a lie? No, he would not do that. Hesitantly, and feeling somewhat foolish, he told the guard about his dream and why he had come all the way to Prague, half expecting the guard to call him a liar and have him arrested.

Instead, the guard started to laugh. "If I had such faith in dreams," the guard said, "I would not be here right now. I, too, had a dream in which a voice spoke to me. It told me to go to the house of a man named Avrom. If I looked under the stove in his kitchen, I would find a treasure, the voice told me. I have heard that half the men in Krakow are named Avrom, and they all have stoves. No, I'm afraid, my foolish man, that you have come all this way for nothing. Instead of finding a treasure here, you have only worn out a pair of your shoes."

Avrom listened in amazement as the captain spoke, describing Avrom's own house. Is it possible that there was a treasure in his own home, hidden where he could not see it? With an eager heart, Avrom hurried back to Krakow. When he arrived home, he dug under his stove right there in the kitchen, and, lo and behold, there was the promised treasure.

Avrom was so happy that he first said a prayer of thanksgiving to God. With some of the treasure he built a house of worship. He kept some of the treasure for his family, and he was able to pay all his debts. And whenever anyone needed help, Avrom remembered his own poverty and offered assistance from his treasure with an open heart.

Like Avrom, many honest, hardworking people who can't seem to make ends meet dream about a way to feed and clothe their children, pay off debts, and, perhaps, shower friends and family with their largess. Unfortunately, life is not a charming old folk tale, and pots of gold are not buried beneath our floorboards. Many of us can get into serious trouble with money, and there's no magical way out.

Good Debt, Bad Debt

Maimonides, the medieval philosopher and physician, said there are three primary sources of evil in the world. First, there is sickness, which is an unavoidable part of nature. The second is the evil we inflict on each other through wars and other acts of aggression. The third is the evil of excess, which we do to ourselves: we eat too much, we drink too much, and we consume too much. "This is the kind of evil all men complain of bitterly," Maimonides wrote, "yet rarely spare themselves, the sort of evil for which the victim is really to blame."

When we live beyond our means, what we are really doing is coveting what others have. And when we covet, we are not only breaking one of God's commandments, we are putting ourselves at risk of going into debt. This is a growing problem today with more people filing for bankruptcy than ever before. From 1992 to 2001, there was a 56 percent increase in personal bankruptcy filings, according to the Administrative Office of the United States Courts.

It's like the story about the philosopher Diogenes, who was sitting on a curbstone eating bread and lentils for his supper. He was seen by the philosopher Aristippus, who lived comfortably by flattering the king. Aristippus told Diogenes, "If you would learn to be subservient to the king, you would not have to live on lentils." To which Diogenes replied, "Learn to live on lentils, and you will not have to cultivate the king."

We charge up on credit cards and borrow from banks in order to live like those we want to emulate. They are like the king for whom we depend on for our sustenance. Consuming makes us happy—until the bill comes. The problem with debt is that it allows money to have power over you because, as the Bible says, "The rich rule over the poor, and the borrower becomes the lender's slave" (Proverbs 22:7).

Many of us accept our financial servitude because it is the American way. I remember an ad for a bank that said, "If you live within your means, you suffer from a lack of imagination." In other words, living on credit is the smart thing to do. According to the bank, it represents an intelligent use of the financial services available to the average consumer. What it really does, however, is promulgate the myth that you can buy things without money.

I'm here to tell you that you cannot buy things without money, even if the banks and credit companies want you to believe that you can. They are in business to make money, and they count on your not being able to pay your debts in full. In fact, the more people are irresponsible about credit, the more credit is extended to them. The credit card companies keep raising the limit when what they should do is cut it off.

Keep in mind that the credit card companies and banks are not your friends. Lending institutions operate legalized loan sharking, only you won't get your legs broken if you can't pay up. You might get a lien on your house, though. And as anyone who has ever had collection agents dogging them for payments knows, being in debt can be a humiliating experience.

When people confess to me about their overspending, they say things like, "I had a bad day, so I shopped." Or, "I had a good day, so I shopped." "It was on sale." They use whatever excuse they can find to rationalize their spending. Yet it's clear that their behavior is similar to other addictions. For some, spending is a mood elevator, like a drug. For others, shopping is a form of entertainment. The mall has become our stage, our park, and our town square. The truth is, overspending is like alcoholism and gambling, which is why there are twelve-step programs for spendthrifts. But, unlike alcoholism, we live in a society that makes overspending attractive and acceptable.

Of course, not all debt is bad. Most of us need credit to buy a home or to send our kids to college. And I'm not saying that you shouldn't occasionally splurge and treat yourself and your family; I'm talking about habitual spending. Are you unable to open your mail for fear of seeing your bills? Do you shop whenever you have a mood swing? If so, there is some other pain in your life that you are trying to cover up. Debt is merely a portal into your feelings of emptiness and dysfunction. It's a portal into your deepest fears and desires. It's about trying to disguise reality.

I discovered my own desire to live beyond my means when my wife and I were remodeling our new home. Because I am surrounded by people who have a lot more money than I do, I found myself overspending in order to keep up with the Joneses and Greenblatts. I wanted my kitchen to look like their kitchen. I wanted my yard to look like their yard. I told myself that I worked hard, so I deserved what other people around me had. You would think that someone in my position would understand that life isn't fair. But I felt, mistakenly, that this was a way to redress the unfairness.

There is usually some event that lets us know that we are out of control, and, for me, it was my inability to pay the contractor. I had to call my father to borrow money, which was an extremely unpleasant call to make. I realized then that my house is never going to be as fine as many of my congregants' houses. So what? That wake-up call put an end to my self-destructive behavior. There's an old saying that rich is anyone with a little more money than you have. Playing catch-up is not only a losing battle, it's a waste of time and it saps your spiritual life from your bones.

Ultimately, we all have to stem our desire to consume as a way to increase our feelings of self-worth. Stop using credit to numb yourself from what is really going on in your life, and be conscious of your behavior so you don't let money and debt have power over you. Unless you treat the underlying reason why you overspend, you are not going to stop overspending for good.

My father used to say, "If you never spend more than you make, you will always have what you need." Charles Dickens, the author of *Bleak House*, also did the math: "Annual income twenty pounds, annual expenditure nineteen six, result happiness. Annual income twenty pounds, annual expenditure twenty pounds ought and six, result misery."

The problem is we are encouraged to buy things we can't afford so that we don't miss an opportunity. If Jeremiah, the Hebrew prophet who lived nearly twenty-six hundred years ago, were alive today, he would ask us, are we learning anything from our actions? Could the time we spend in the mall be better spent doing other things? Do we really want to spend the limited time we have here on Earth shopping? What are we teaching our children by letting them see us buy things we can't really afford?

Learning good spending habits should start in childhood. My kids get a ten-dollar allowance each week, if they've been good. As soon as they've saved up enough to buy something, we go on a shopping trip. When my son tells me he would like a CD, I say, "You have your own money, buy it." He sees that he has twenty dollars, just enough for two CDs, and, because he's a kid, he buys them both. Now he's broke. The next time we are in a store, he asks me for a new toy. "You spent your allowance," I remind him.

"Can't I pay you back next week?" he pleads.

"Nope, you have to wait until you earn more."

Although I could lend him the money, that would

teach him that he can get whatever he wants whenever he wants it. I want my children to learn that even though we have the ability to buy on credit, it is better to wait until we actually earn the money to pay for it. Children are more comfortable when they understand their limits; adults should be as well.

Keeping Our Word

When we borrow money, be it from a friend, family member, or bank, we are signing a promissory note or making a verbal agreement to pay the lender back. When we renege on our debts, we are breaking a moral code.

Consider the priest who stood outside his church one Easter Sunday with the doors locked. As the time for the evening mass approached, a crowed gathered on the steps. People were anxious to get to their seats and begin, but the priest refused to let them in. Soon there were hundreds of people pressed up against each other outside the church doors.

"Father," one of the parishioners finally shouted, "why won't you open the doors?"

"I can't let any of you in," replied the clergyman. "There's no room left in the sanctuary."

"That's impossible," the man said, challenging the priest. "Every member of the congregation is standing here outside. How could the sanctuary possibly be full?"

"It is full, all right," the priest stated. "Full of all the promises, all the lofty intentions, all the silent vows you left behind the last time you were here. Not one of you took them with you when you left this holy place."

Keeping our vows is important. My kids know how seriously I take swearing an oath by subjecting me to a little test. When they were younger, before they could do the math, I would try to convince them that I had dated whoever the most recent pop star was when I was in high school. Britney Spears? "Yeah, sure, I went out with her." Jennifer Lopez? "Took her to the prom." The kids would howl and laugh and protest and tell me they knew I was making it up. No matter what, I'd stick to my story. Until they pulled out their secret weapon. The one thing that always made me fess up and tell the truth.

"Daddy, do you swear on the Torah that it's true?" Even in jest, my kids know that I can't swear on the Torah unless I really mean it. Sadly, it seems like this sort of fidelity to the truth, to being God-like in our words and our deeds, is rare these days. But keeping our word can be the most fundamental way by which our character is judged.

Consider this remarkable true story that occurred in the aftermath of World War II. A tall, young Army lieutenant's heart was pounding as he waited by the big round clock at Grand Central Station in New York. He was waiting to meet the woman who had been on his mind for the past thirteen months, the woman he had never seen, yet whose written words had kept him alive in his darkest moments of fear. In one of his letters, he confessed to her that he often felt afraid.

"Of course you fear—all brave men do," she answered. "Didn't King David know fear? That's why he wrote the Twenty-third Psalm. The next time you doubt yourself, I want you to hear my voice reciting it to you."

And he did imagine her voice before facing the fear of

battle, and it did renew his strength. Now he was going to hear her real voice. She would be wearing a small, red rose in her suit lapel so that he could recognize her.

He thought back to the book that the Lord must have put into his hands out of the hundreds of Army library books sent to the Florida training camp where he was stationed. It was called *Of Human Bondage,* and, throughout the book, there were margin notes in a woman's handwriting. He was astonished that a woman could see into a man's heart so tenderly. Her name was on the bookplate: Hollis Meynell. He got hold of a New York City phone book and found her address. He wrote. She answered. The next day he was shipped overseas, but they continued to correspond. For thirteen months they wrote. Now, he believed he loved her and she loved him.

But she had refused all his pleas to send him her picture. "Suppose I'm beautiful," she wrote. "Then I would always worry that you cared for me only because of my beauty. Suppose I'm plain (and you must admit this is more likely). Then I'd fear that you were writing me only because you were lonely and had no one else. No, don't ask for my picture. When you come to New York, you will see me and then both of us are free to stop or go on after that."

When the clock struck six, a young woman came toward him. She was tall and slim; her auburn hair lay back in curls. Her eyes were as blue as flowers, her lips and chin had a gentle firmness. Her pale green suit was like springtime itself. He started toward her, completely forgetting to look to see if she was wearing a rose in her lapel. As he moved toward her, a small, provocative smile curved her lips. "Going my way, soldier?"

That's when he saw Hollis. She was standing directly behind the woman in the green suit. She was well past forty, her graying hair tucked under her worn hat. She was plump, her thick ankles thrust into low-heeled shoes. But she wore a red rose in the rumpled lapel of her brown coat.

The lieutenant wanted to follow the young girl, but there stood Hollis. Her pale, plump face was gentle and sensible. Her gray eyes had a warm, kindly twinkle. The lieutenant did not hesitate; he gripped the worn copy of the book he carried to identify himself. This would not be love, but perhaps a lasting friendship for which he must be forever grateful.

He squared his shoulders, saluted, and held the book out toward the woman. "I'm Lieutenant John Blandford, and you must be Miss Meynell. I'm so glad you could meet me. Can I take you to dinner?"

The woman's face broadened in a tolerant smile. "I don't know what this is all about, son," she said. "That young lady in the green suit, the one who just went by, begged me to wear this rose on my coat. And she said that if you asked me to go out to dinner with you, I should tell you that she's waiting for you in that big, Italian restaurant across the street. She said it was some kind of a test."

Everyone who hears this story loves it. It's a moving example of honor, romance, and love. But what if it was a story not about keeping a promise to have dinner, but about keeping a promise to repay an actual debt? Would we still find it so touching? Probably not. For some reason, we don't tend to see repaying our debts as achieving the same level of honor and moral importance as other forms of keeping a promise.

We are tested each day. Each time we say, "I'll be there," "I'll call you back," "it's a deal," "you have my word." We're tested each day by our children, who remember our promises, broken or kept, for the rest of their lives. We are tested, too, when it comes to our word and money. If you want to judge a person's character, judge whether or not that person keeps his or her word when it comes to money. Promising to repay our debts and doing so is one of the most basic, fundamental aspects of what it means to be a good person. Time and time again I have seen families and friendships torn apart because of a failure to repay a debt. Don't let it happen to you.

CHAPTER SEVEN ‖ # Our Brother's Keeper

I DO NOT CARRY ANYONE ON MY SHOULDERS TO TAKE HIM TO THE FINAL GOAL. NOBODY CAN CARRY ANYONE ELSE ON HIS SHOULDERS TO THE FINAL GOAL. AT MOST, WITH LOVE AND COMPASSION, ONE CAN SAY, "WELL, THIS IS THE PATH, AND THIS IS HOW I HAVE WALKED ON IT. YOU ALSO WORK, YOU ALSO WALK, AND YOU WILL REACH THE FINAL GOAL." BUT EACH PERSON HAS TO WALK HIMSELF, HAS TO TAKE EVERY STEP ON THE PATH HIMSELF. HE WHO HAS TAKEN ONE STEP ON THE PATH IS ONE STEP NEARER TO THE GOAL. HE WHO HAS TAKEN A HUNDRED STEPS IS A HUNDRED STEPS NEARER THE GOAL. HE WHO HAS TAKEN ALL THE STEPS ON THE PATH HAS REACHED THE FINAL GOAL. YOU HAVE TO WALK ON THE PATH YOURSELF.

—BUDDHA

‖ W HEN IT COMES TO FAMILY
and money, things can get ugly. Consider the joke about
Ralph, who was on his deathbed, and his brother, Charlie, who was by his side. They both had worked together
for years in the family's garment business.

"Charlie, I have a terrible confession to make," Ralph
said weakly. "I want to repent for my sins."

"What could you have done that was so bad?" Charlie asked.

"Remember when someone stole two hundred fifty
thousand dollars from our company while you were on
vacation? It was I who took the money."

"That's all right," soothed Charlie. "This is no time to
think of things like that."

"And when you created that new pattern that would
have put us ahead of other garment-makers in the country, it was I who stole the drawings and sold them to our
competitor before our own company could get it on the
market."

"Never mind. Try to rest," said Charlie, patting his
arm.

"But Charlie, I was the one who convinced your wife
to leave you so that I could marry her and get even more

of your money," Ralph said, sobbing with remorse. "Oh, Charlie, I'm so sorry. Please forgive me before I die!"

"What's to forgive?" answered Charlie. "I'm the one who poisoned you! We're even."

Yes, family businesses sometimes can get ugly, and my family's business was no exception. I have only seen my father cry once in the past twenty-five years. It happened recently when we were sitting on the couch in my den talking about this very book. My father grew up poor. When my mother met him, his family was on public assistance and he owned only one pair of pants. He wore them to work, came home, took them off, washed them, and then put them on to see my mom in the evenings.

I wanted to know from my dad how his parents handled money during his impoverished childhood. I wanted to know the story behind the story about his parents not talking to him for years because of some argument over money. My dad's not a hyperbolic guy. He tells it like it is—nothing more, nothing less. So he sat me down and told me the story of Leder Brothers Scrap Iron and Metal.

Unfortunately, in many ways, his story is not unique. He grew up in a family business. It's how many of our grandparents made it in America. Scrap iron, dry goods, produce, cattle: it's all the same idea. Start small, save your pennies, employ the family, buy low, sell high, grow, and, hopefully, prosper. In one or two generations, these small businesses provided the cash flow to mold many of us into what we are today—educated, relatively affluent, successful Americans. Or did it? I suppose it's all a matter of what we mean by successful.

Dad and my Uncle Mort started by picking metal out

of the garbage at the dump and taking it to the local scrap yard for a few bucks. At that point, they were young boys working for their father. My grandfather was an ignorant, Russian peasant who fled to America to avoid conscription in the czar's army. He worked his sons to the limits of their teenage physical capabilities. He didn't think twice about slapping them around every once in a while, and he kept virtually all the money they made, which wasn't much.

My father and uncle eventually fell in love with women they wanted to marry. After they wed, they needed more money to start families. My grandfather was unyielding. They got what they got and that was that. So my dad and Uncle Mort decided to break away from their father and branch out on their own. From that point on, my grandparents refused to speak to them. This went on for years.

It was "do or die" for the newly formed Leder Brothers Scrap Iron and Metal Company. Dad and Mort bought an old truck and started servicing accounts. They didn't even have a building at first. A friend let them park the truck in his coal yard; they worked outside, suffering from frostbite when the Minnesota winters turned cold. With no place to lock up their tools at night, they piled coal on top of them and then dug them out each morning. Dad and Uncle Mort took the jobs no one else wanted, such as wrecking cast iron boilers and copper pipes out of burned out and condemned buildings. Eventually, they bought a little piece of land and put up a shed to stay warm. They bought more trucks and serviced more accounts.

They managed to buy a double lot in the suburbs, build two houses side by side, raise, clothe, feed, and educate their children. Eventually, they started buying up some of the condemned buildings from the insurance companies. Then, they started buying and developing newer properties. After twenty years, Dad and Uncle Mort had made it. But the more they made, the farther apart they seemed to drift. These two brothers needed each other, but after witnessing so many arguments between them when I was growing up, I didn't know if they actually loved each other. Dad and Mort eventually became brothers, business partners, and next-door neighbors whose wives and children rarely interacted. I remember listening to them argue about who did what to whom, about who was lazy, who really made the money, who screwed up the deals gone bad, and where the stapler belonged on the desk.

I became a rabbi in part because I fled this family business. I didn't want to pay that sort of psychic price for every dollar I earned. Eventually, as they grew older, my grandparents started speaking to their sons again. But truth be told, there was an anger and ache that never really went away. The final insult came when my grandfather died and left my father only five dollars in his will. My father wept as he told me this part of the story. He was crying not for the money—he had done very well on his own—but for the pain caused by losing a father all in the name of money.

The fact is, money, whether you have it or you don't, can be the cause of familial jealousy and strife. I can't tell you how many times I've counseled mothers and daughters, fathers and sons, brothers and sisters, whose relationships were torn asunder because of money. Gary, for example, lent his sister money, which she has never paid back. He's never felt the same about her since. He hasn't cut himself off from her, and he still sees his niece, but there will always be a cloud over that relationship. Gary is willing to live with that cloud in order to keep the family intact.

Sadly, not everyone is able to set aside his or her money disputes for the sake of the family. Cheryl and Diana were once inseparable. They shared a room growing up, choosing to remain in their hometown so that they could live close to each other. The trouble started when Cheryl borrowed one thousand dollars from Diana, who owns her own public relations firm. Cheryl was between jobs and needed help paying her rent. Diana was happy to do it, believing that she would be paid back as soon as Cheryl found a new job. But when it came time to pay back the loan, Cheryl said, "Why should I pay you back? You don't need the money. You can afford it!" Diana and Cheryl no longer speak.

For Rachel, who borrowed money from her mother, Sarah, so she could buy a used car for college, it was a case of a convenient memory loss. After graduation, when Sarah asked her now-employed daughter to begin repaying back some of the money she had loaned her, Rachel was aghast. She told her mother, "That wasn't a loan you gave me, it was a gift!" Sarah responded by cutting her daughter off completely.

These kinds of disputes, if not settled quickly, can escalate from hurt feelings to anger, and, quite often, a cold war. As Shakespeare's Polonius said, "A loan oft loses both itself and friend." And while I believe it is our obligation as humans to help those in need, lending money can be a risky venture, and there are smart ways to lend money so that you protect both your cash and, more importantly, your relationships.

Even Abraham Lincoln understood this when he wrote the following letter to his stepbrother in 1848.

Dear Johnston:

Your request for eighty dollars, I do not think it best to comply with now. At the various times when I have helped you a little, you have said to me, "We can get along very well now," but in a very short time I find you in the same difficulty again. Now this can only happen by some defect in your conduct. What that defect is, I think I know. You are not lazy, and still you are an idler. I doubt whether since I saw you, you have done a good whole day's work in any one day. You do not very much dislike to work, and still you do not work much, merely because it does not seem to you that you could get much for it.

The habit of uselessly wasting time is the whole difficulty, it is vastly important to you, and still more so to your children, that you should break this habit. It is more important to them, because they have longer to live, and can keep out of an idle habit before they are in it, easier than they can get out after they are in.

Let father and your boys take charge of your things at home—prepare for a crop, and make the crop, and you go to work for the best money wages, or in discharge of any debt you owe, that you can get. And to secure you a fair reward for your labor, I now promise you that for every dollar you will, between this and the first of May, get for your own labor either in money or in your own indebtedness, I will then give you one other dollar.

By this, if you hire yourself at ten dollars a month, from me you will get ten more, making twenty dollars a month for your work. In this, I do not mean you shall go off to St. Louis, or the lead mines, or the gold mines in California, but I mean for you to go at it for the best wages you can get close to home in Coles County.

Now if you will do this, you will soon be out of debt, and what is better, you will have a habit that will keep you from getting in debt again. But if I should now clear you out, next year you will be just as deep as ever. You say you would almost give your place in Heaven for seventy dollars or eighty dollars. Then you value your place in Heaven very cheaply, for I am sure you can with the offer I make you get the seventy or eighty dollars for four or five months' work. You say if I furnish you the money you will deed me the land, and if you don't pay the money back, you will deliver possession.

Nonsense! If you can't now live with the land, how will you then live without it? You have always been kind to me, and I do not mean to be unkind to you. On the contrary, if you will but follow my advice, you will find it worth more than eight times eighty dollars to you.

Affectionately,
Your brother
A. Lincoln

Abraham Lincoln's matching fund was a brilliant strategy for helping his slacker stepbrother out of debt without giving him a handout. He didn't refuse him a loan, but he did devise a plan by which his relative would be motivated to work.

SAY IT. WRITE IT. MEAN IT.

Unlike Lincoln's well thought out personal contract with his stepbrother, most lending problems occur when there is a lack of clarity during the initial transaction. As difficult as this is to do with relatives, it is essential to be clear about what is being asked for and what the terms are for repayment. As I said in my chapter on debt, I borrowed a large amount of money from my father to help refurbish our new home. But when I asked my dad for the money, I told him I would forgo receiving the money he and my mother give to each of their five children each year until the debt was repaid. It was clear from the very beginning when he would get his money back. Because it was my father, we had a verbal agreement, but it doesn't hurt to put it in writing, even with a blood relative.

If a family member asks you for a loan, tell the borrower that you love them and you want to help, and that you don't want this loan ever to ruin your relationship. To prevent there ever being a misunderstanding in the future, write down what the deal is so that there's no room for misinterpretation years from now. I don't think this is an unreasonable conversation to have. It's usually easier if the person doing the borrowing suggests writing down the terms.

A good way to deal with lending money, especially if you have some doubt about the person's ability to pay you back, is to offer to be a co-signer at a bank. This creates a layer of protection by making the bank the lender and not the family member. You can say, "I don't want to lend you the money personally because I don't want this to become a problem later on, but I'm happy to go with you to the bank to co-sign a loan." Being a co-signer prevents the borrower from being beholden to the family member when it comes time to pay the loan back. Now, you can still get stiffed if the borrower is unable to make the bank payments, but it removes the emotional dynamic from the transaction, which is helpful in avoiding resentment. It's the bank asking for the money, not you.

It's not so much, in the case of the wealthy person, that the lender needs the money, but they need to know that they can trust the relationship. Not paying back a loan is a violation of that relationship. It's a violation of good faith. If your child took a quarter out of your purse without asking, you would confront him, right? It's not about your need for the quarter, it's about teaching your child to respect and honor your property and his word.

When it comes to repaying loans, whether or not the lender needs the money back is irrelevant. Repaying a loan is about keeping your word. Broken promises destroy relationships. It's a character issue.

Whenever I lend my children money, I expect them to pay me back the same day. When they do, I take a moment to say, "Thank you very much for paying me back. It's very important to pay people back when they lend you money. You've done a good thing." By letting a loan slide with your children, the message is that they don't have to pay people back. We all want to be generous with our kids, but it's even more important that we teach them the value of independence and keeping a promise.

If you've lent money to a sibling, for example, who is not paying you back, you are now dealing with a web of relationships that includes the in-laws, parents, and other siblings. Don't let a year go by hoping that you will get your money. Like any relationship, letting something go that is bothering you is foolish. Don't get the other members of the family involved. Make a phone call to your sibling after a few months have gone by without payments and say, "Listen, I was expecting some of the money I lent you, so I'm calling to remind you to get it back to me on time."

If the borrower tells you he or she doesn't have the money, you're essentially sunk, unless you have a written agreement and you want to throw the relationship away by going to court or getting someone (unrelated) to mediate. The question now becomes, how important is this relationship to you?

The fact is, money changes the dynamic of all relationships. If you must borrow from or lend money to a family member, be clear and, above all, keep your word. Once again, it's not about money. When you don't make good on your word, you lose your trustworthiness. If a relative is kind enough to lend you money, you have a moral obligation make good on your promise. Acts of kindness deserve to be rewarded by keeping your word. And if you are in the midst of a dispute about money, ask yourself if you are going to let this issue destroy one of the strongest bonds we have as humans.

Remember Cain and Abel? They were the brothers who offered sacrifices to God. When Abel's sacrifice was accepted by God and Cain's was not, Cain became enraged and killed Abel. Then God asked Cain a question. "Where is Abel?" To which Cain responded, "How should I know? Am I my brother's keeper?"

This story has been misinterpreted as a way to absolve us of responsibility for helping a family member. "I am not my brother's keeper," the common phrase now goes. But the story is really a cautionary tale about what *not* to do and how *not* to behave. Of course we are our brothers' keepers. But we also have every right to expect our brother to keep his word.

GET OVER IT

No matter what issue has broken apart a family, especially if it's about money, we must learn to forgive. What family doesn't have issues, be they greedy thoughts about inheritance and property, a power struggle in the family business, or grownup kids who always have their hand out? It's all about power, status, and the position in the family hierarchy. My grandfather wasn't able to forgive his sons, and his sons weren't able to forgive each other. Our imperfect families bring out the worst in us, and yet, somehow, we know there is no other group of souls anywhere on Earth who care more for and about us.

Consider the Bible story about two brothers, Jacob and Esau. For twenty years, Jacob and Esau had not seen one another. The rift occurred after Jacob duped his brother out of the only thing he really had—not money, but the birthright blessing of their blind and dying father, Isaac. For twenty years, Jacob had been running from himself and from the shame of what he did.

Suddenly, word came to Jacob that the mighty Esau was on the march with four hundred men. Soon the parched, jagged desert would be quenched by the blood of his brother's revenge. Jacob quickly divided his family into two camps. If Esau attacked one, at least the other would escape, he reasoned. He sent the servants ahead to greet Esau with gifts. Poor Jacob still thought everything could be bought—even forgiveness.

Night fell, and the only thing left to do was wait and tremble in the darkness. In the morning, Jacob saw Esau in the distance, marching forward with his troops. Jacob bowed low to the ground seven times and awaited the final death blow. What did the mighty Esau do when he saw Jacob? He broke from the other men and looked into his little brother's eyes. He hugged him and he kissed him.

He wept. The mighty Esau was strong enough to forgive. After all the years of jealousy and anger, when they looked into each others' eyes, they were still brothers who hugged, who kissed, who wept, and who forgave.

Cain and Abel, Jacob and Esau, my father and Uncle Mort—all brothers who let petty jealousy and competition get in the way of their relationship. All of them lost precious years of love due to jealousy and money. We should follow, instead, the example set in the well-known legend of two other brothers who were farmers. One lived with his wife and children on one side of the hill, and the other, unmarried, lived in a small hut on the other side.

One year the brothers had an especially good harvest. The married brother looked over his fields and thought to himself: "God has been so good to me. I have a wife and children, and more crops than I need. I am so much better off than my brother, who lives all alone, is. Tonight, while my brother sleeps, I will carry some of my sheaves to his field. When he finds them tomorrow, he'll never suspect that they came from me."

On the other side of the hill, the single brother looked at his harvest and thought to himself: "God has been kind to me. But I wish He had been as good to my brother. His needs are so much greater than mine are. He must feed his wife and children, yet I have as much fruit and grain as he does. Tonight, while my brother and his family sleep, I will place some of my sheaves in his field. Tomorrow, when he finds them, he will never know that I have less and he has more."

So both brothers waited patiently until midnight. Then each loaded his grain on his shoulders and walked toward the top of the hill. A few minutes after midnight, they met one another at the hilltop. When they realized that each had thought only of helping the other, they embraced and cried with joy.

Two brothers with two different means. But somehow, they managed to see beyond their own lives and appreciate each other's struggle. I thought of them and their devotion to family above money when I was asked to make a house call to visit a man named Ben.

"My Dad was never religious, but he said he'd like to see a rabbi before he dies," his son and only child, Mark, told me over the phone. "He has cancer, and he's living with me and my family now. He has no place else to go, and he can't get out any more."

The address was up a winding canyon—an urban Los Angeles winding canyon—traffic whizzing by, houses packed up against each other like so many kernels on an ear of corn. The front yard was brown and weedy with a broken sprinkler and a folding chair off to the side. I knocked, and Mark let me in.

"Dad, the rabbi is here," Mark said loudly over his shoulder. "He's in the living room on the couch—go ahead, Rabbi."

Mark looked much older than when I last saw him. I'd officiated at his wedding some five years before. Now, he was gray and balding. He was tired. When I found Ben, his father, on the couch, I knew why. He and Mark shared the same birthday. They shared the same apartment, and later, the same house. When Mark was young, Ben used to come home late from work some nights, wake Mark up, bounce him in his bed, and toss him in the air. Then, "one, two, three—up we go!" onto the kitchen counter, feeling ten feet tall, to dip graham crackers in cold milk. Sometimes, Ben gave Mark a bath.

Ben's wives had all left him. His first wife threw him out for losing all their money on scams. His second wife threw him out for the same reason. That's when Ben moved in with Mark. Ben could sell anything. In the seventies, he was the guy who showed up on your front door step to sell you a vibrating bed. Just give him a second to set up the demo model in your living room. In the eighties, it was shoes. In the nineties, oil well investments. Ben always believed that wealth and power were just around the next corner. All he had to do was mortgage the house to get here. The deal was always a con, and Ben was the chump.

But Ben had a joke for every occasion. He was down and out so often that he had a special place in his heart for anyone in trouble. He couldn't do a favor for you fast enough once you asked him. He was a snappy dresser, he could fly a plane, and, man, could he dance.

Now, Ben was in the last stages of lung cancer. His skin was thin, spotted, and brittle as a dead leaf in the fall. His body was mostly bones, and his face was so gaunt, his eyes seemed too large for his head. I sat next to him, yet a universe away, in my navy suit, crisp white shirt, polished shoes, and dimpled tie. Ben looked at me in his diaper, gray sweat pants, and undershirt with a leak proof pad and a round, foam cushion beneath him. He had no idea who I was or why I was there.

Although he wasn't in pain, every gesture, syllable, and word took more strength than he had to spare. I wanted to help Ben . So in my most compassionate rabbi's voice, I said, "Ben, I'm the rabbi. I know you wanted to see me. How can I help?"

Ben slowly rotated his head in my direction, locked in on me with his huge, brown eyes, and whispered, "I have to take a crap."

I said I was there to help, I thought to myself, but there's a limit. You want to talk theology, you want to pray together, you want to plan your funeral with me— I'm game. You want me to change your diaper—I'm out. I went to find Mark. "Uh, I think he has to go to the bathroom," I said timidly.

Mark sighed and headed toward the living room. I pulled back to watch a remarkable moment unfold as slowly as a flower. "Okay, Dad," Mark said facing his father on the couch and bending over. "Put your arm around my neck. Come on, Dad."

With Mark's help, Ben managed to put both of his stick-like arms around his neck and lace his fingers together. "On the count of three, Dad. One, two, three—up we go! Don't let go," Mark reminded Ben as he slowly lifted him off the couch so that they were now face to face. Ben's body slumped against Mark's. His arms still locked in place behind his neck. Mark's arms were around Ben's waist.

Then, the dance began: the most tender dance I had ever seen. "That's it, Dad," Mark encouraged, as he slowly rocked from side to side. Ben shuffled each foot, still grasping onto Mark with all his strength. Ever so gently, Mark inched him toward the bathroom where Ben could lie down to have his diaper changed. "That's it.

Good, Dad. Now I know why Mom said you were such a great dancer." Side to side, inch by inch. The old man and his middle-aged son, holding on to each other against the sadness and the ache—swaying to the melody only they could hear. Ben died a week later.

Mark and Ben's story is both sad and sweet. So often, I have seen families' stories that are entirely sad without any of the sweetness. So often, the source for much of that bitterness is money. Mark and his wife could have let money ruin the last days of their lives together with Ben. But they chose a better way. There are no perfect families. But at the end of the day, and at the end of our lives, we can't let money come between us. We can't let anything come between a hug, a kiss, and the melody only we can hear.

CHAPTER EIGHT

Loss Does Not Mean Lost

"MONEY IS ALWAYS THERE, BUT THE POCKETS CHANGE; IT IS NOT THE SAME POCKETS AFTER A CHANGE, AND THAT IS ALL THERE IS TO SAY ABOUT MONEY."

—GERTRUDE STEIN

‖THE ANCIENTS BELIEVED IN
the power of curses. The Bible is filled with them. Disobey
God, and you could be struck down by consumption,
fever, inflammation, plagues, locusts, and a host of other
blights. The curses are so horrid as to be almost laughable
to a modern reader, but they were no joke to our
ancestors.

One of my favorite Yiddish curses is, "May you be
like a chandelier: hang by day and burn by night." And,
"May you grow so rich that your widow's second husband never has to worry about making a living!" Sure, we
laugh at the idea of curses, and maybe even blessings. But
as ridiculous as they may sound, I think people, in a
sense, believe in them.

I see a lot of life and death in my job. When people
are in pain my phone rings. When they lose their jobs,
their marriages, and their loved ones, it's me, and thousands like me, to whom people turn for answers. The
truth is everyone suffers sooner or later. Whether or not it
is literally the case, everyone feels damned or cursed at
some point in their life.

There's the humorous story about a deeply depressed
man who felt that his life was cursed. He was miserable at

home with his wife and children. He couldn't concentrate, so his work suffered. He went to see his doctor to see if he could get some medication. After examining the man and listening to his complaints, the doctor said: "What you need is not medication, but a good laugh. Take your wife to the theater to see Carlini the comedian. He packs the house every night. His jokes convulse the crowd."

"But, doctor," the patient cried, "I *am* Carlini."

Like Carlini, many good people do feel cursed by life, and in a way, all of us are. There's an old proverb about a woman who lost her husband. She told her rabbi that her bereavement robbed her of all peace of mind, and that her friends' efforts at consolation merely increased her sorrow. The rabbi advised her to bake a cake using ingredients gathered only from the people in the town who had never experienced loss.

The anguished woman went from door to door, but each time she was unable to get even a single grain of flour. That night, weary with disappointment, she returned to the rabbi to report her failure. Suddenly, it dawned on her that the failure was the remedy. She realized that she had not been singled out, but rather that sorrow is the fate of all mortals.

We all experience the pain of loss at some point in our lives. Losing a loved one is the worst, of course, but losing money also can be debilitating. Maybe you got creamed in the stock market or you made a bad business investment. Perhaps your savings were drained in a divorce, or you were laid off or fired. Some people have had money stolen, while others frittered away their own money by gambling or overspending.

LIFE AFTER LOSS

Whatever the reason, the loss of money can mean a drastic change in one's life. Such is the case for Salvatore Nardulli of Staten Island, New York. After thirty years of working for the airlines, the fifty-three-year-old Nardulli lost his job as part of industry cutbacks. He still hasn't found a full-time job after more than a year of searching. His wife, Lorraine, has been equally unsuccessful in her attempts to find work as a legal secretary, a job she has done for years. The once-middle-class couple can no longer afford to pay their rent, car insurance, phone, or electric bills. And if things don't get better soon, they will be forced to go on welfare.

No one knows for sure how many people are in the same situation as the Nardullis, but the number of Americans who have exhausted their unemployment benefits, about 1.5 million, is the highest in two decades, according to Department of Labor statistics.

And though it's difficult to find a silver lining after losing your income, loss of any kind teaches us that we can only control so much in life. Because we are human, we are limited in our ability to control certain events. We have control over how much we spend and how much we save, but we can't control the economy. We can't prevent a crisis from taking place. Things happen to us that we simply cannot predict or change.

I've found that people react to loss in one of two ways. There are those who rail against it and remain bitter for the rest of their lives, and there are those who make peace with it and understand that loss is a part of life and that life can be rediscovered in loss. The latter are the ones who become wise instead of bitter. They are ones who are able to handle both future successes as well as failures.

There is a difference between being wise and being smart, and it takes a certain kind of wisdom to handle loss. Many people, like the Nardullis, lost their jobs after September 11, 2001. Companies have merged, downsized, or gone completely out of business. As I said in my chapter on work and money, losing a job is much harder to deal with than losing money because jobs are so often linked to identity. If I lost my job, for example, but didn't lose my money, I still would be unhappy because who I am in the world is so highly connected to what I do.

Losing a job is especially difficult for men. When men meet, the first question they often ask each other is, "What do you do?" not "What are your interests?" And men draw a whole host of conclusions from the answer. Is he more or less successful than I am? Is he smarter, more important, or more powerful? The same is true for many professional women who have a great deal of emotional investment in their jobs.

Because most of us spend more time at work than we do at home, when we lose a job, we are also losing a second family. And for those who are entrepreneurs, losing a business is like losing a piece of themselves. Even the Talmud says, "It would be better for a man not to have been born at all than to experience economic dependence upon others."

Victor Frankel made the most important point of all about choices in the midst of adversity in a brilliant book called *Man's Search for Meaning*. A concentration camp survivor and psychotherapist, Frankel says we have choices no matter how dire the situation. We can be humane to one another by sharing our bread, or we can be selfish and think only of our own needs. The choices we make during the most trying times reveal our real values as human beings.

Loss is an opportunity for change. It's a chance to wipe the slate clean and start all over, if you want to do so. Above all, it's an opportunity to discover the love and support of your family and friends.

Rick Meyers, a friend and former neighbor, learned this after the real estate business where he worked went belly up during the early nineties. At the tender age of thirty, Rick, who was in charge of the company's finances, was able buy a $1 million home in Los Angeles for his wife and two children. His kids went to exclusive, private schools, and he and he and his wife took luxurious vacations and ate out often at the best restaurants in town.

All that changed after the business collapsed. The Meyers lost everything, including their home, and Rick's parents had to move into a condo so his family could live in their three-bedroom house. "This was the worst period of my life," Rick recalled. "There was the humiliation of having to file for bankruptcy, but mostly I was unbelievably scared. I remember one month when I didn't have a red cent in my bank account. I just stared at the bills in terror. I nearly lost it that day, but luckily, I had just gotten a four hundred dollar refund check from my insurance company—just enough to scrape by with the bills. I remember feeling how lucky I was to get that check in the mail."

Yet, all through this tremendous ordeal, the Meyers never gave up hope and they were able to find strength in each other. "Failure was not an option for me," Rick said. "Not with two kids. We tried to maintain some semblance of our former lifestyle, which I believe saved our sanity. We allowed ourselves to go out every now and then, not to expensive restaurants, of course, just so we could get out of the house and forget our troubles for an hour or two. And with all the difficulties that that we faced, my wife and I had a tacit understanding that we would do everything we could to get out of this mess and to support one another. There were times when I was in tears and she would comfort me, and vice versa. I don't know what I would have done without her."

With the help of a brother and a friend, Rick was able to start his own financial consulting business. "I had a brother who was doing well, but I was reluctant to ask him for help, even though I knew I would help him out if he were in the same situation. I finally got the nerve to ask, and he and a dear friend of mine lent me some money so we could pay our debts and get back on our feet."

And though his life is not as opulent as it once was, he has a solid business, and he is now debt free. "Since I run my own business, no one will be able to fire me or take my business away from me ever again. We haven't accumulated any wealth, but we have no debts and we are living well."

Sadly, many people who have lost it all are not as fortunate as Rick. They don't have family or friends who can come to the rescue, and they feel as though they are alone. They see a world in which everyone appears luckier and more successful. The fact is no one is immune to adversity. Being human means we will sometimes feel pain. Loss by itself is neutral. It can do almost anything to us. It can make us bitter and resentful, or make us hard and cruel. It can plunge us into despair and futility. But loss does only what we allow it to do. There are people like Rick to whom loss comes sharp, deep, and dark, and yet they find a way to turn their sorrow into a blessing—their ache and sadness into a renewal of strength.

MAKING LOSS MATTER

The real tragedy of life is not that we suffer pain and disappointment, but that we sometimes learn nothing from it. Not only are we never alone in our sorrow, but the suffering we feel after a loss can be transformative if it is imbued with meaning. If we can find a purpose in our misfortune, we will triumph over our adversity. I'm not dismissing the heartbreak we feel, but a loss can reveal something deep and meaningful about how we want to live our lives.

Asking, "Why me?" is the wrong question. It's an understandable question, but it's a cul de sac with no way out. We have to move from the "why?" to the "what?" and the "how?" *What* are we I going to do with the rest of our life? *How* are we going to live now?

A man once stood before God, his heart breaking from the pain and injustice in the world, and said, "Dear God, look at all the suffering, the anguish and distress in your world. Why don't you send help?" God responded, "I did send help. I sent you." Like Rick Meyers, if we have lost money or are unemployed, we must do whatever it takes to get back on our feet, but we can do so by drawing ever more deeply from the well of love in our marriage and family.

To those who lost it all by gambling or cheating others, both Christians and Jews believe in repentance. We believe people who have made mistakes can apologize for them and be forgiven by God by changing their behavior and their lives. Christians call this absolution; Jews call this *teshuva*, which literally means, "to turn." Sometimes it takes a crisis for us to wake up and change.

People come to me who have embezzled in their business or squandered their family's or clients' savings. Joey Golding is one of those people. A former multimillionaire who worked as a Beverly Hills money manager during the greed-is-good decade, Joey is an example of someone who was able to learn from his mistakes. He sought my counsel after he was caught cheating his clients. As president and owner of a brokerage firm, Joey was charged by the Securities and Exchange Commission, the FBI, and the U.S. Attorney's Office in California with operating a fraudulent trade allocation scheme, whereby he assigned profitable trades to certain customers and losing trades to others. Golding allegedly directed the trading of millions of dollars in seventy customer accounts.

"I was on the cover of the *Wall Street Journal* and *Money* magazine, but I was so empty inside," Joey told me of his high-flying days. "I actually stood by a newsstand to see if anyone would recognize me, that's how shallow I was. When my business blew up and me with it, I lost my wife and my money, as well as my reputation, which wasn't worth very much to begin with. I found that I was left with just me and what was inside me. I was forced to see what Joey Golding was really like. It took years of intensive therapy to put myself back together again. I had a lot of faith in myself and God, and the only opinion that was important to me was my own."

After serving time in prison and taking a long, hard look at himself, Joey discovered that being a multimillionaire wasn't his true calling after all. In 1996, Joey founded a nonprofit organization that provides dinners, clothing, and blankets for the homeless, seniors, and people with disabilities. He went from zero to hero, even earning honors from George W. Bush.

"It turned out that losing my business was the greatest thing that could have happened to me," he says, "because it put me on the path that I was meant for in life. Half the harm that is done in this world is due to people who want to feel important. They don't mean to do any harm, but they are absorbed in the endless struggle to make it big. I now know that money is something that rents space in your pocket. When I'm seventy-five, I'm going to remember the people whose lives I've helped, not how much money I've made."

But I'm not dishonest, you say. I'm a hardworking, decent person who lost everything. Why did this happen to me? There's an old joke about a guy who goes up to heaven and meets God. He says, "God, I was a good person my whole life and you struck me down with this terrible disease. I lost my family and I lost all my money. Why did you do this to me?" God looks at the man and says, "Who are you?"

In other words, we are not the center of God's universe. I believe humanity is, but not individual human beings. Dispossess yourself of the idea that being a good person will prevent bad things from happening to you. As one rabbi said, "That's like expecting a bull not to charge you because you're a vegetarian."

Then why be good, you might ask? Because being good, like charity, is its own reward. There is no cosmic accounting system. Goodness does not protect you from evil. What goodness does is make you the kind of person who can cope with misfortune, if it happens to you. Have you ever noticed that kind, generous people are always surrounded by friends who care?

To those who blame their misfortunes on God, I say, God is not in the business of picking and choosing who suffers and who doesn't. I don't believe in that kind of supernatural intervention. Once we accept this, we will be able to move on because we are not seeing ourselves as victims. God had nothing to do with our personal problems. Those of us who have experienced a loss will discover what kind of people we are by whether or not we see ourselves as victims.

If you have friends or family who are struggling due to a loss of a job, the best thing you can do is to anticipate their needs and to be there. Don't say, "Let me know if you need anything," because that places the burden on the sufferer rather than on us. Like Woody Allen said, "The single most important thing in life is showing up." Time and time again I hear it from those who are hurting. The simplest gestures matter.

Abraham and Moses, two of the Bible's greatest

figures, were called by God. Each answered the same way: "Here I am." We, too, are called by God to reach beyond our own lives and to care about the sorrows of others. Sometimes it might be to talk about someone's fears, to take them out for lunch or dinner, or just to listen. Sometimes a little creativity is in order. Offer to look at their resume, introduce them to someone you know in a similar business, volunteer to baby-sit for the kids so they can go to an escapist movie.

Prayer also helps. I don't believe praying to God prevents troubles from occurring because I don't believe God is the cause of a crisis. But I do believe that prayer unlocks tears and hidden sorrow. Prayer helps the healing process. Prayer pierces the isolation around us with the swaying, songs, and comfort of our words. Prayer is hope. Hope is knowing that someone is making an effort to help. Hope is knowing that friends and family are not far away. Hope is picking up the pieces and trying again.

My first date with the woman who is now my wife lasted twelve hours. We started with dinner and ended up talking until the sun rose over the Ohio River the next morning.

What made Betsy so interesting to me and made me fall in love with her was more than her perfect azure eyes and shy smile. It was her suffering. Betsy seemed to understand pain and heartache. She seemed wise beyond her years. When the wind blew, I discovered why. The breeze moved Betsy's hair enough for me to see a bald spot in the back of her head. "I lost it from radiation," she told me. Betsy went on to explain that she had just finished treatment for Hodgkin's disease, a dangerous but curable cancer.

People who have struggled are more interesting, more mature, and have more to say than those who walk through life unwounded. Why? Because they are less wasteful of time and love, less foolish and confused. Sure, it would be nice to be born with wisdom, but I haven't met a person yet who was.

The most important lessons can only be learned through struggle: until we have been disappointed by life, we will never know humility or fearlessness. Everyone gets wounded. We all walk through life with some kind of limp. Loss is life's challenge to us to wrestle meaning and purpose from our sorrow, recognize that within our wounds is pain, but so, too, the secret of becoming truly blessed.

| # Being Truly Rich

"A BURIAL SHROUD HAS NO POCKETS."

—YIDDISH PROVERB

‖A COUPLE CAME TO SEE ME recently because they were thinking about not having their son become a bar mitzvah. They said they didn't want to participate in the crass materialism that extravagant bar mitzvah parties often represent. I told them that instead of denying their son this marvelous rite of passage, they should look at it as a chance to show him what their values are as a family. Sit him down and tell him, "Even though we can afford to give you a large party, we are choosing to have an intimate gathering. We would like to focus on the ceremony, which we consider the real celebration." What an amazing opportunity.

Another couple that came to see me was having trouble deciding whether to have a big wedding or to use some of that money for a down payment on a house. The woman wanted the big, fancy wedding and the man wanted the house. A fight ensued and they were ready to call the whole thing off. My job was to get them to see that planning their wedding would help them decide what they really stood for as a couple in their marriage. This was the first of many decisions that would test their ability to achieve something together while holding onto their fundamental values.

"Close your eyes and tell me how you see yourselves ten years from now," I asked the bride-to-be.

"I see a house filled with children," she said.

"If this is what marriage means to you," I told her, "then don't get wrapped up in the big wedding fantasy. You won't be reminiscing about your flowers, gown, or wedding gifts ten years from now." Another opportunity!

A successful woman at whose wedding I officiated five years ago came to see me. Her husband had to close his entertainment business after the economy went south. She told me that she was secretly resentful of him because she now saw him as a failure.

I told her, "You must ask yourself what your husband needs from you right now. You need to think about him and not about yourself. This new challenge will enable you to understand what it means to be a good wife." She realized that she was feeling like a victim and that her husband was suffering far more than she was. Once again, opportunity knocked.

All of these examples illustrate how money can bring out the best and worst in us. It can bring out our most negative traits, but it can also give us the opportunity to discover what is truly important in our lives. Whether we have money or we don't, it is essential to be thoughtful about what money means to us and to accept the challenges that it brings. We all have a sense of right and wrong that we've inherited from our faith and families, and money is one of the chief ways we put our morals to the test. Decisions about money are never really about money itself: they are about something deeper. They are not about our professed priorities and values, but our true priorities and values. Remember, money itself is only a tool, a way of expressing what's important to us. How we spend our money and how much of our time we are willing to expend in order to have more money is a true reflection of our inner selves.

THE REAL BOTTOM LINE

I realize it is difficult not to devote time and energy to acquiring goods when we're encouraged by our culture to do so almost every waking moment of our lives. I also understand that some of what I suggest in this book will take a great deal of effort to do because it requires changing the way we think as well as the way we live. But if you use the following Ten Money Commandments as practical and moral guideposts, I promise that you will be richer in mind and in spirit:

Rabbi Leder's Ten Money Commandments

1. NET WORTH DOES NOT EQUAL SELF WORTH.
   Stop equating what you earn with your value as a person. The true measure of a person has precious little to do with money.

2. IT'S NOT ABOUT THE MONEY.
   Whatever our issues are concerning money, they are probably masking a deeper, more profound problem. Try to figure out what's really going on while changing your negative money behavior. See a

therapist if you think it will help you to get to the root of your problem.

3. **UNDERSTAND THE DIFFERENCES BETWEEN YOUR WANTS AND NEEDS**
Are you a slave to excess and materialism? Do you have an insatiable set of wants? Ask yourself if you really *need* whatever it is you want the next time you go shopping.

4. **DON'T LIVE BEYOND YOUR MEANS**
Remember that you cannot buy things without money, even if the banks and credit companies want you to believe that you can.

5. **TEACH TRUST, NOT JUST TRUST FUNDS**
While we all want our children to have a financial cushion, give them a legacy of values in addition to an inheritance. Remember that the time we spend with our kids is more important than the money we spend on them.

6. **STOP WORKING YOUR LIFE AWAY**
Are you working seven days per week? Give yourself a day for rest and reflection by keeping the Sabbath or setting aside some time for prayer or meditation.

7. **SAVE YOUR RELATIONSHIPS BY BEING CLEAR WHEN LENDING MONEY**
If a family member or friend asks you for a loan, offer to be a co-signer at a bank instead. Even if you don't use the bank as an emotional buffer, make sure you write down the terms of your agreement to

avoid problems later on. If things still don't work out—learn to forgive. Losing your family over money isn't worth it.

8. **DON'T LET MONEY BREAK YOUR HEART**
In marriage, money is an opportunity to create a shared vision for your life together. It doesn't have to be a deal breaker or a heart breaker.

9. **RECEIVE BY GIVING**
Joseph Campbell said by giving to those who are less fortunate, money is like congealed energy, "and releasing it releases life's possibilities."

10. **LEARN TO BE GRATEFUL**
God has created an abundance of what we need most (food, family, and love), yet we often fail to see how well our needs are taken care of. Be grateful for the daily manna we already have. Over and over again when people come to see me who are suffering in some way, be it cancer, a divorce, a loss of any kind, they wish they could rewind their lives. Why? Not only to go back to a time before their troubles began, but also to go back in order to appreciate the things they took for granted. When sorrow comes, it's the simple things we miss most—laughter, the company of friends, the sun, the rustling of leaves.

There is a beautiful passage from a prayer book that says it best: "Sometimes it seems that day after day, and week after week, we go about the earth seeing nothing. Wonders without number surround us, but we are oblivious. Our eyes are open, but our sight is dulled by petty concerns. We yearn for wisdom, yet miss the opportunities for enlightenment all about us. So let us pause a while, open our eyes and contemplate the wonders we overlook."

What Counts?

Last year, one of my confirmation students returned to Los Angeles after a semester abroad in South America. I asked her what the biggest difference was between the village she visited and where she lives in Los Angeles? "People are happier there," she said without hesitation. "They have much less than most of us, yet they celebrate more. They sing and dance more. Their families eat together. People take care of each other when they're sick, and they help their neighbors when they are in trouble."

How often do we sit down to eat as a family? How many of us know our neighbors, let alone reach out to them when they are in trouble? When was the last time you sang and danced? What is true wealth, if not friends, children, family, and a life spent helping and cherishing others?

There was a man who acquired his wealth through hard work and by performing good deeds. He was proud of what he had accomplished. One day he called his ten sons close to him and told them, "My children, I will one day soon distribute my wealth among you while I still live. You will each receive one hundred gold pieces. You should not have to wait for my death in order to benefit from this money. Even though I remain alive, you will have full control of the money and can use it any way you please."

Time passed and the man's fortune turned. Soon the man found himself with only 950 gold pieces left to him. He called his ten sons to his side once again and said, "My children, a portion of my fortune has been lost, but I want to keep the promise that I made to you some time ago. I promised to give each of you one hundred gold pieces, and I can still do that, but only for nine of you. From the fifty remaining gold pieces I must keep thirty for myself and for my burial expenses. That leaves only twenty gold pieces for one of you.

"I am, as you know, blessed with ten good friends, companions of my youth, and they will be friends to the son who chooses to inherit the remaining twenty gold pieces. Since it is difficult for a parent to choose, I will ask you to choose; which one of you will volunteer to become the possessor of the twenty coins?"

The father looked at his sons one by one. Each son in turn lowered his eyes and shook his head. Finally, the father turned to his youngest son—the one he had secretly loved the most.

"Yes, Father, I will be content with the twenty gold pieces, and I happily accept your offer," the youngest son said as he lovingly embraced his father.

"Good," answered the father. "But know that my friends will be your companions, and they are worth more than gold and silver."

A short time after that, the father died. The sons observed the traditional seven days of mourning. Then the nine sons, without a thought for the youngest brother, began to spend the money their father had given them. Soon they had spent their entire inheritance.

Meanwhile, the youngest brother remembered his father's words about his ten friends. He called on each of them, saying, "Before my father died, he asked me to keep you as friends, and I want to honor my promise to him. I am about to leave this village to seek my fortune elsewhere. But before I go, I would like to invite you to a farewell dinner. Please come so that you may help me keep my word to my father." The friends all accepted his invitation with great pleasure.

At the modest dinner, the friends engaged in lively conversations, each one in turn telling a story about their friend, the young man's father. At the end of the dinner, one of their friends stood up and said: "Dear friends, we are all recalling our old friend with such great love. And of all his sons, only his youngest has kept his memory alive by remembering his companions. Why should we also not respect our friend and honor him by helping his son? Why should this loyal young man have to go far away from our community to be with strangers in order to earn a living? Let us each contribute a generous sum of gold and help him establish a business here in our midst!"

All the other friends cheered in agreement, and so it was done. The young man became a prosperous merchant and always treasured these friends of his father's as his own, recalling his words: "My friends will be your companions and they are worth more than gold and silver."

The value of friendship is a simple truth that we all know on some level, but we bury this knowledge in the hustle bustle of our lives and in our pursuit of material wealth. The value of time is another truth often lost in the hurry and the worry of our modern-day lives.

Today is our second chance. Today is the day to stop wishing for a better life and to start making one. Don't wait until it is too late to be grateful for what you have. Have we spent enough time with our spouse and children? Do we lose our temper with our elderly parents? Do we abuse our body with too much food and drink? Do we abuse our mind with too much television or gossip? Do we abuse the Earth with our careless waste? Do we really do something for the poor and hungry? Do we at least grant them the dignity of looking into their eyes? Are we fair in business when we could cheat without being caught? Are we kind to strangers whom we will never see again, in line, in traffic, on the telephone?

These are simple acts of goodness, but they are ultimately what make our lives and others' richer. Just ask Marian, who has been battling cancer for a year now. She might make it and she might not. It's been a tough, ugly year. But it's also brought out the best in her. She's a better person for the fight and she knows it.

Not long ago it was Marian's sixty-fifth birthday. A group of her friends and family, all of whom she's learned to love and appreciate like never before, threw a party for her. When it came time to blow out the candles, Marian quietly crossed her fingers and made a wish. Everyone in the room knew what it was. She wanted another year— just one more year. Marian craves the future. She cherishes it and believes in it. What kind of future do we want for ourselves and our children?

A few years ago, I was called to see an extremely

famous and wealthy movie director. He was a friend of a friend, and he was in the hospital. We were strangers, this dying old man and I. Entering his room, I noticed amid the monitors, tubes, and florescent lights of the sterile ICU, there was only one solitary breath of humanity tacked up on the wall—one small black and white photograph, some sixty years old, of a young couple in their twenties holding hands on a park bench.

I entered the room, glanced at the photograph, and then focused on the balding, white-bearded man behind the oxygen mask. His name was John. With a curl of his hand hanging limply off the side of the bed, he motioned me toward him, removed his oxygen mask, and tried to speak. Too weak, he replaced the mask, closed his eyes, rested, and tried again. Again and again he tried. A whisper. A mumble. "John, I can't understand you," I told him, "but I'm not leaving until I do. So, rest and we'll try again in a few minutes."

Finally, pulling me gently down over the bed, John pressed his dry lips against my ear and mumbled a simple question: "What is it all for?"

Suspended in a moment both eternal and brief, there we were. The dying seeking an answer, the answer of answers, while holding a stranger's hand; a stranger who was supposed to know. My eyes darted to the little black and white picture, then back to John, laboring for breath. And with Zen-like clarity that surprised me, I uttered a response as simple as his question. "It's to love and be loved," I told him. "They understood that," I added, pointing to the photo.

"You're right," John whispered as he closed his eyes

and drifted off to sleep. In a way, I felt sorry for John. With all of his success, he was dying alone, asking a stranger what life was really about. I believe what I told him. A life well lived is filled with love given and received, the ebb and flow of time and generosity.

No matter what our net worth, all of us can become rich with family, caring, and laughter. We can all invest in and achieve the wealth of friendship. We can all spend less time counting our money and more time counting our blessings. We can all lead richer lives, ever more grateful simply to love and be loved.

‖ Suggested Reading

Brooks, David. *Bobos in Paradise: The New Upper Class and How They Got There*. New York: Simon and Schuster, 2000.

Canfield, Jack and Mark Victor Hansen, eds. *A 3rd Serving of Chicken Soup for the Soul: 101More Stories to Open the Heart and Rekindle the Spirit*. Chicken Soup for the Soul Series. Edison, New Jersey: Health Communications, Inc., 1996.

Dickens, Charles. *Bleak House*. Reprint, New York: Penguin Classics, 2003.

Frankl, Viktor. *Man's Search for Meaning*. Boston: Beacon Press, 2000.

Fulghum, Robert. *It Was on Fire When I Lay Down on It*. New York: Villard Books, 1989.

Fulghum, Robert. *Uh-Oh: Some Observations from Both Sides of the Refrigerator Door*. New York: Random House, 1995.

Greenberg, Sidney S. *A Treasury of Comfort: A Source of Consolation, Hope, Courage and Guidance for Those Who Mourn*. North Hollywood: Wilshire Book Company, 1978.

Beth Ann Krier. "Her Tin Can Overfloweth: $2.5 Million for Charity," *Los Angeles Times*, 11 September 1986, p. 1.

Kushner, Harold. *How Good Do We Have to Be?: A New Understanding of Guilt and Forgiveness*. New York: Little, Brown and Company, 1996.

Max, Aggie. "The Bag Lady and the Banquet," On *Salon.com*, *www.salon.com/july97/mothers/aggie970722.html*. Originally

184 || MORE MONEY THAN GOD

published in *The Last Resort: Scenes from a Transient Hotel* (San Francisco: Chronicle Books, 1997).

Menchin, Robert. *101 Classic Jewish Jokes: Jewish Humor from Groucho Marx to Jerry Seinfeld*. Memphis: Mustang Publishing, 1997.

Mundis, Jerrold. *Making Peace with Money*. Kansas City: Andrews McMeel Publishing, 1999.

O'Neill, Jesse H. *The Golden Ghetto: The Psychology of Affluence*. Milwaukee: The Affluenza Project, 1997.

Schram, Peninnah. *Jewish Stories One Generation Tells Another*. New Jersey: Jason Aronson Inc. Publishers, 1996.

Spalding, Henry D., ed. *Joys of Jewish Humor*. New York: Random House, 2000.

‖ Permissions

‖ About the Author

AFTER RECEIVING HIS DEGREE IN WRITING from Northwestern University and studying at Trinity College at Oxford University, Rabbi Steven Z. Leder received a master's degree in Hebrew Letters in 1986 and Rabbinical Ordination in 1987 from the Hebrew Union College Jewish Institute of Religion in Cincinnati.

Rabbi Leder currently serves as senior rabbi at Wilshire Boulevard Temple in Los Angeles and teaches homiletics to rabbinical students at the Hebrew Union College Jewish Institute of Religion.

He received the Louis Rapoport Award for Excellence in Commentary by the American Jewish Press Association and the Kovler Award from the Religious Action Center in Washington, D.C., for his work on African American and Jewish relations. He is a fellow in the British American Project, a think tank devoted to bringing together influential leaders from America and Great Britain.

Rabbi Leder's first book, *The Extraordinary Nature of Ordinary Things,* spent two weeks on Amazon.com's bestseller list for Los Angeles and Beverly Hills, resulting in national acclaim. He has appeared on several networks, including two appearances on ABC's *Politically Incorrect* and several on National Public Radio.

Most important of all, he is married to Betsy Leder and is Aaron and Hannah's dad. He is also a Jew who likes to fish. Go figure.